AF228901

JEWISH MEDAL OF HONOR RECIPIENTS

WILLIAMS-FORD

TEXAS A&M UNIVERSITY

MILITARY HISTORY

SERIES

JEWISH MEDAL OF HONOR RECIPIENTS

American Heroes

MICHAEL LEE LANNING

Texas A&M University Press

COLLEGE STATION

This paper meets the requirements of ANSI/NISO Z39.48–1992 (Permanence of Paper).
Binding materials have been chosen for durability.

Manufactured in the United States of America

Library of Congress Cataloging-in-Publication Data

Names: Lanning, Michael Lee, author.
Title: Jewish Medal of Honor recipients:
American heroes / Michael Lee Lanning.
Other titles: Williams-Ford Texas A&M University military history series.
Description: First edition. | College Station: Texas A&M University Press,
[2022] | Series: Williams-Ford Texas A&M University military history
series | Includes bibliographical references and index.
Identifiers: LCCN 2021050030 (print) | LCCN 2021050031 (ebook) | ISBN
9781648430367 (hardcover) | ISBN 9781648430374 (ebook)
Subjects: LCSH: Medal of Honor—Biography. | Jewish soldiers—United
States—Biography. | World War, 1914–1918—United States—Participation,
Jewish—Biography. | World War, 1939–1945—United States—Participation,
Jewish—Biography. | Korean War, 1950–1953—United
States—Participation, Jewish—Biography. | Vietnam War,
1961-1975—United States—Participation, Jewish—Biography. | United
States—History—Civil War, 1861–1865—Participation, Jewish—Biography.
| BISAC: HISTORY / Military / United States |
HISTORY / Reference | LCGFT: Biographies.
Classification: LCC UB433 .L375 2022 (print) | LCC UB433 (ebook) | DDC
355.1/3420922—dc23/eng/20211028
LC record available at https://lccn.loc.gov/2021050030
LC ebook record available at https://lccn.loc.gov/2021050031

CONTENTS

PART 3. Medal of Honor Recipients, Possibly Jewish

PART 4. Medal of Honor Recipients Incorrectly Identified as Jewish

JEWISH MEDAL OF HONOR RECIPIENTS

Introduction

THIS INTRODUCTION IS by no means the definitive guide on how to identify who is or is not a Jew, nor is it a history of Judaism in general. Rather it serves as a primer to the ill-informed about the Jewish religion and its followers. It also offers readers a glimpse into the difficulties involved in the identification and labeling processes. These complexities do not, however, in any way diminish the bravery or self-sacrifice exhibited by those Medal of Honor recipients included in this book. Nor does it diminish the bravery or self-sacrifice of any service member who is or has been incorrectly identified. Bravery is bravery. Self-sacrifice is self-sacrifice.

Despite all best efforts, there may be recipients omitted from this book who, in fact, were or are Jewish; likewise, there may be included recipients who were or are not indeed Jewish.

As a result, this book contains four sections. First, it focuses on the seventeen Medal of Honor recipients who are without a doubt Jewish. The second section, with explanations, includes those thought to be Jewish but for whom there is no conclusive proof. A third category identifies medal recipients who might be Jewish. Finally, the last section spotlights those who earned the medal but, based on conclusive evidence, were incorrectly identified as Jews.

Recipients of the Medal of Honor form the smallest group of veterans of the US Armed Forces as well as one of the most exclusive organizations in the United States. The purpose of this book is to recognize the uncommon valor of a few members of this body. The best explanation of the inclusion of these Jewish heroes is stated in the Introduction to *Fighting for America: An Account*

of Jewish Men in the Armed Forces from Pearl Harbor to the Italian Campaign,
published by the National Jewish Welfare Board in 1944. It states:

> They were all selected for this volume because they are Jews. Yet, if this fact
> were not stated plainly, or if their names were disguised, they might have
> been any other group in America, or of any other religious faith because
> basically their war experience, their battle courage, their contributions
> to victory were, in character and in degree, the same as that of other
> Americans at the battle fronts. They were moved by the same motives,
> defending the same principles, drawn into battle by the same laws, trained
> in the same military establishments, sustained by the same heritage of
> freedom and democratic experience.

The primary obstacle in recognizing the valor of Jewish Americans—dating
from our country's founding to the present—is identifying and defining just
who is a Jew. Judaism is not a race, ethnic group, or even a separate culture.
It is a religion. However, that is where simplicity ends. Although Judaism is
a religion, a person does not have to practice its observances or even believe
in a God to be a Jew. Generic dictionaries define a Jew as a descendant of the
Hebrew people and/or an adherent to Judaism. More specialized sources
expand the definition of Judaism to specify that the Jews are people who are
born into a Jewish family or who have some Jewish ancestral background,
particularly on the matrilineal side. Yet being a Jew is not limited to birthright
only. Individuals with no Jewish background can convert to Judaism and be
just as Jewish.

Jews who practice Judaism—whether born into the faith or converted—
follow beliefs, traditions, practices, and ethics based on the Torah. The Torah
(the Teaching, or the Law) contains the first five books of the Hebrew Bible,
which are traditionally written on a scroll wound around two wooden poles.
On a historical level, the Torah records the story from the creation of the
world to the death of Moses in about 1200 BCE. On a moral level, it provides a
guide to living for those who practice Judaism. The Torah has 613 Commandments categorized into 10 Decorations, these latter being the equivalent of the
Christian Ten Commandments.

Both following the tenets of the Torah and inheriting Jewish ethnicity
make one a member of the tribe that began with the union of Abraham and
Sarah some 4,000 years ago—the tribe that came out of Egyptian slavery,
according to the Book of Exodus, as "Hebrews" or "Children of Israel." These

Children of Israel, so named for their region of origin, were actually twelve tribes, ten of which were dispersed by the Assyrians in 722 BCE. The other two, the tribes of Judah and Benjamin, remained in their homeland that became known as Judea. In 586 BCE, the Babylonians invaded and conquered Judea and exiled the survivors, who became known as Judahites, which translates from the Hebrew to "Jew." The religion of the Judahites became known as Judaism.

From that time until the middle of the twentieth century, Jews lived scattered around the world without a homeland. While they adapted to their new homes and adopted the norms of their neighbors, they maintained—to varying degrees—the tenants of Judaism, proudly declaring themselves Jews no matter where they lived. These "varying degrees" of Judaism ranged from Orthodox to Liberal. Orthodox Jews believe that God literally gave Moses the Torah and that it, word by word, remains valid and true today. Liberal Jews are more likely to believe that, while the Torah is divinely inspired, it has been defined and redefined by Jews through the ages according to the times and locations.

Dividing Jews into the categories of Orthodox and Liberal is but a start to providing accurate descriptions to those who follow Judaism. Orthodox—which itself means "proper doctrine" or "correct belief"—followers range from those who wear black coats and hats and avoid many modern conveniences to those with similar beliefs who dress in jeans indistinctively from their neighbors.

Liberal Jews divide themselves into multiple subgroups, including the Reform Jews, which are the largest component of the faith in the United States. They believe that all Jews should make all decisions, physical and spiritual, based on their conscience rather than laws as outlined in the Torah. They believe in following the writings of the prophets; they emphasize education and success. Reform Jews do not necessarily wear yarmulkes or prayer shawls, and in 1972 they were the first Jews to ordain women as rabbis. They also accept someone as Jewish who has a Jewish father only.

Conservative Judaism beliefs lie between those of the Orthodox and Reform Jews. Like the Orthodox, they observe Shabbat (the seventh day of the Jewish week, the day of rest and abstention from work as commanded by God) and other holidays; say daily prayers; and keep kosher. At the same time, they agree with the Reform Jews that all traditions and practices should be reviewed and reconsidered with the passage of time.

There are also other groups of Jews with varying beliefs and practices. Reconstructionists, members of a separatist movement that started in the late 1920s, basically believe that God is not a being but rather is nature itself. They see rabbis as facilitators rather than leaders. The Jewish Renewal is a recent movement that draws its belief from a broad number of sources ranging from the Torah and prophets to environmentalism and gender equality. Humanistic Judaism, established in 1963, defines Judaism as the cultural and historical experience of the Jewish people and encourages Jews, both humanistic and secular, to celebrate their Jewish heritage by participating in Jewish holidays, weddings, and bar and bat mitzvahs.

The groups that deviate from traditional Jewish practices have fewer than 100 synagogues combined, but they offer insight into the complexities defining a Jew because so many of the faith do not fit common stereotypes. Other than the black garments, yarmulkes, and prayer shawls worn by some Jews, there are no other visual indications of those who follow Judaism, including their appearances. Political cartoonist of the last century attempted to identify Jews by the Semitic features of exaggerated noses and ears. While that lineage applies to some and is surely the root of anti-Semitic labels, Jews as a tribe are not themselves Semitic people—that is a classification that belongs to Arabs and Assyrians as well as Jews. Further, all Jews are not by any means Semitic but rather followers of Judaism that include Africans, Asians, and Hispanics as well.

Each synagogue is separate and distinct from others. Unlike Catholics, who have their pope as their leader and other religions who have a single senior pastor or priest, there is no overall head of Judaism. Jews are a tribe with many families and many families of many beliefs.

Ultimately, this great diversity of Jewish beliefs makes it difficult to identify who is or is not a Jew without documentation. In the military one would expect identification would be in service records. This is not the case for many reasons. Prior to World War I, military records were brief with often incomplete handwritten notations. Neither those kept by the state nor federal governments recorded a person's religion with any consistency. Furthermore, some Jews, in order to avoid anti-Semitism, made no claim as to religion when they enlisted or were drafted. Many US Army veteran records, both those that recorded religion and those that did not, were destroyed in a fire in 1973 at the St. Louis, Missouri, military records center. Personal identification tags, commonly called dog tags, did not become standardized with name, service number, and religion until World War II. Even then many Jews—especially those fighting in Europe and risking capture by the Germans—did not want the *H* for Hebrew on their tin tags.

The most readily available proof of a person's being a Jew should be, of course, their membership and attendance at a synagogue. One of the most definitive forms of identification as a Jew would be burial under a Jewish headstone in a Jewish, often named Hebrew, cemetery. Yet death and burial records do not account for Jews who do not keep the traditions of Judaism, who have totally left the tribe to convert to some other religion, or who have no beliefs at all. Jews can also be identified by their own assertion or those by their surviving families. However, many of families of Jewish servicemen, especially those who served in the first half century after the medal was authorized during the Civil War, are difficult—if not impossible—to trace. Claims by historians and other writers about a person being a Jew can be somewhat helpful, but those claims are often not documented or, unfortunately, prove to be inaccurate. Genealogical records, including birth and death certificates, and census data, especially for those who have been dead for some time, may at times reveal religious beliefs.

Jewish surnames can be another indication of a person being a Jew, but not all Jews have Jewish surnames and not all those with Jewish surnames are Jews. Many soldiers who served in the US Armed Forces during and before World War II were immigrants with Germanic surnames that have been mistaken as having Semitic origin. In other cases, difficult-to-spell immigrant names were shortened or Americanized by immigration officials. Still others do not have Jewish surnames because of marriage, conversion to the religion, or happenstance.

Even so, Jews and their Judaism have survived because of their ability to adapt and change with the passage of years. Over the centuries, Jews and Judaism have had many enemies and few friends, but they have endured and prospered. At present there are approximately 6 million Jews in the United States, 5 million in Israel, and a total of another 15 million spread around the world.

In the end, identifying a person as a Jew comes down to a case-by-case record search. Every effort has been made to properly identify those Jewish heroes who have earned the ultimate award for service to their country.

Jewish American Military History

JEWS HAVE BEEN AN integral part of the American military since before the United States won its independence. They have fought in every war and conflict to protect the liberties and freedoms of their country. In doing so, many Jewish Americans have earned the highest decoration for valor awarded by the United States of America—the Medal of Honor.

Since colonial times, Jews have served in the US military in numbers that represent a higher percentage than their percentage of the overall population. They have participated in every major battle and in every war, standing—and often falling wounded or killed—in defense of their fellow service members and preserving the liberty of their country and that of freedom-loving people around the world.

Jews have long been on the North American continent, being among the first European explorers of the New World. The earliest Jews were crewmen for Christopher Columbus's 1492 voyage, being "Maranos," a sect of Jews living on the Iberian Peninsula who, during the Middle Ages, had converted or had been forced to convert to Christianity; yet they continued to practice Judaism in secret.

The first verifiable contribution of Jews to what would become the United States occurred in 1654 in New Amsterdam (the future New York City). In that year Asher (also spelled Asser) Levy and twenty-two fellow Jews immigrated, mostly from the Caribbean and South America, to the newly established village on Manhattan Island. In 1655, Peter Stuyvesant, the governor of the Dutch colony, and his council issued an ordinance "that Jews cannot be permitted to serve as soldiers, but shall instead pay a monthly contribution for their exemption."

Levy and his fellow Jews wanted to serve in their local militia and provide security for their village. They resented having to pay a tax to *not do* something they wanted to participate in. Levy and his comrades petitioned the local government for "the right to fight." Their request was initially rejected, with the officials commenting if the Jews did not like the law, they could go elsewhere. Levy said, "I have not asked to be exempted. I demand the right to stand guard." After appeal all the way back to Holland, the Jews of New Amsterdam were permitted to serve with and fight on an equal basis as their fellow colonists.

There were few Jews in North America during the early colonial period, but those who were present made significant differences. Isaac Myers formed a company in New York in 1754 and captained the unit during the French and Indian War. That same year George Washington led an expedition across the Alleghany Mountains to Pittsburgh. His journal of the expedition mentions two Jews as members of his command.

When the American colonists rebelled against Great Britain, there were about 4 million residents of the North America colonies. Only about 3,000 were Jews, but at least 160 rallied to the cause of freedom and independence. These Jews served at all levels from enlisted rifleman to senior officers. Col. Isaac Franks served as Gen. George Washington's aide-de-camp, and Solomon Bush advanced in rank to become the deputy adjutant general of the Pennsylvania militia. Baltimore merchant and politician Solomon Etting wrote in 1824 that Jews in the military during the Revolution "were always at their posts and always foremost in all hazardous enterprises."

Soon after the successful conclusion of the American Revolution, Washington and other leaders realized the need for a military academy to educate and train future officers. Simeon Magruder Levy was one of the two men who composed the first graduating class in 1802 of the US Military Academy at West Point.

While the official records of Jewish participation in the War of 1812 are meager because the British captured and burned much of Washington, DC, including military files, in August 1814, Jews contributed to the continuation of the United States. Capt. Sydney G. Gumpertz, Medal of Honor recipient during World War I, wrote in his 1934 book, *The Jewish Legion of Valor*, "The old fire of the Maccabees was in the hearts of the Jews at the outbreak of the second war with England in 1812. They showed fierce zeal, military skill and dauntless valor. In antiquity, the Jews fought many a stern fight under valiant champions. In America, they furnished generals and fighting men for her forces. The Jew has never been found wanting in patriotism."

Brig. Gen. Joseph Bloomfield commanded US ground forces in a district containing Pennsylvania, Delaware, and western New Jersey for most of the War of 1812. Jews also served their country at sea, with Uriah P. Levy becoming the first Jewish commodore, commanding his ship at sea and establishing regulations that affected the entire navy. His tombstone notes his greatest accomplishment: "He was the father of the law for abolition of the barbarous practice of corporal punishment in the Navy of the United States."

The navy named a destroyer in Levy's honor in 1942. In 2005 the Commodore Uriah P. Levy Center and Jewish Chapel opened at the US Naval Academy at Annapolis, Maryland.

Jews fought and died for lands of North America that were not yet a part of the United States. In 1836 four of the approximate 250 men who died defending the Alamo in Texas were Jews. In the Mexican War that broke out a decade later, Jews once again stepped forward to take up arms for their country. Gen. David Camden de Leon earned the title of "the fighting doctor" when, although his assignment was as a medical officer, he twice led cavalry charges after commanding officers had been killed or wounded.

The Jewish population of the United States increased with migration from Europe, primarily Germany, of Jews fleeing violence and increased anti-Semitism during years prior to the American Civil War. At the outbreak of the conflict, about 150,000 of the total US population of 30 million were Jews. Although they numbered only one half of one percent of the total population, Jews actively participated on both sides. An estimated 10,000 Jews served in the war—some 7,000 wearing the blue of the Union and 3,000 donning the gray of the Confederacy. A total of about 600 from both sides died during the conflict.

The American Civil War pitted brother against brother. It also pitted Jew against Jew. American Jews felt a stronger bond to their state and neighbors than to their religious brothers. Jews residing in the North were strongly pro-Union while those in the South remained loyal to Dixie. Although anti-Semitism was still rampant, both sides promoted Jews to high-ranking positions in both the military and in government. Jews in both blue and gray earned the stars of generals and the eagles of colonels. Judah P. Benjamin, a nonobservant Jew, served as acting secretary of war of the Confederate states. When the United States authorized the Medal of Honor early in the war, Jews were among the first recipients.

Gen. Oliver O. Howard, commander of a Union corps and the Army of the Tennessee during the Civil War, was known as the "Christian General" because he attempted to base his policy decisions on his deep religious beliefs. Oliver wrote after the war, "I can assure you, my dear sir, that, intrinsically, there is no more patriotic men to be found in the country than those who claim to be of Hebrew descent, and who served with me in parallel commands or more directly under my instructions. I have always greatly esteemed the Jewish people and in fact, the highest hopes I have in the future are derived from him whom I think justly claimed the spiritual king of the Jews. So far as bravery is concerned, bravery often carries rashness. History affords no superior those of the Maccabees and other leaders of the Jews, back to the time of Jacob, the prince, who prevailed with God."

That is not to say, however, that there was a total lack of anti-Semitism during the war—even with the dead. When post-battle cemeteries were opened in Spotsylvania Court House and Fredericksburg, local officials did not want "Jewish boys" buried there. As a result, Jewish dead from those two fights, as well as from the Wilderness and Chancellorsville battles, were taken to Richmond and buried in the city's Hebrew Cemetery. By war's end, thirty Jews, including three officers, rested in a plot that became known as the Hebrew Confederate Cemetery, the only Jewish military cemetery outside of Israel in the world.

Confederate brigadier general Thomas N. Waul of Texas said, "Jewish soldiers were brave, orderly, well-disciplined, and in no respect inferior to the gallant body in which they formed a prominent part. Their behavior in the field was exemplary and no Jew was ever before a court martial. I never heard of any Jewish soldier shirking or failing to answer any call of duty or danger."

Jews continued to serve in the postwar US Army. They participated in the Reconstruction of the South and battled Native Americans on the western plains. Fifteen Jewish sailors died on the USS *Maine* when it blew up and sank in Havana Harbor on February 15, 1898. The Jewish executive officer of the *Maine*, Adolph Marix, survived the blast and went on to become a vice admiral.

In the Spanish American War that followed the sinking of the *Maine*, about 5,000 Jews served on land and at sea. A sixteen-year-old, Jacob Wilbusky, a volunteer in Col. Leonard Wood's and Lt. Col. Theodore Roosevelt's Rough Riders, was the first casualty in the battle for San Juan and Kettle Hills. Roosevelt promoted five men, including one Jew, for bravery in the battle. Thirty Jewish army officers and twenty naval officers served in the conflict.

Jews also served on the other side of the world during the Spanish-American War. Sgt. Maurice Joost, one of 100 Jews in the 1st California Volunteer Infantry Regiment, was the first casualty in the attack on Manila in the Philippines.

More than 250,000 Jews entered the US Armed Forces by volunteering or through the draft during World War I. About 3,500 were killed and more than 12,000 wounded. They earned at least 1,100 valor decorations.

Gen. John J. Pershing, commander of the US Expeditionary Force, said of Jews serving in his command, "When the time came to serve their country under arms, no class of people served with more patriotism or higher motives than the young Jews who volunteered or were drafted and went overseas with our other young Americans to fight the enemy."

Jews, motivated both by love of their country and the rising awareness about the treatment of Jews by Nazi Germany, again stepped forward in World War II. More than 550,000 Jewish men and women joined the services, of whom about 1,100 were killed and 40,000 wounded. In addition to the Medal of Honor recipients detailed in this book, another 157 received the Distinguished Service Cross, and 1,600 earned the Silver Star.

Gen. Mark W. Clark, commander of the United States Fifth Army in Italy said, "Thousands of Americans of the Jewish faith are serving under my command, carrying their share of the burden in battle in Italy. Many of them have been killed in the service of their country. To American soldiers of the Jewish faith goes my most sincere thanks for their faithfulness, diligence, and bravery in battle. To those who have passed on must go a nation's gratitude."

In the Pacific Theater, Gen. Douglas MacArthur said, "I am proud to join in saluting the memory of fallen American heroes of the Jewish faith."

The service of Jewish sailors in World War II was recognized by Adm. Harold R. Stark, commander of the US Navy in Europe, who said at the end of the conflict, "The officers and men in the United States Naval Forces in Europe, join to honor those gallant Americans of the Jewish faith who, during this past year, have laid down their lives for their country. We mourn them as brothers—brothers who cannot be with us to share this European triumph toward which they gave their lives."

Jewish Americans have continued to step forward to defend their country since World War II. About 150,000 Jews served in the Korean War and 30,000 in the Vietnam War. During those decades, Adm. Hyman G. Rickover became known as the "Father of the Nuclear Navy," and Adm. Jeremy M. Boorda rose from the enlisted ranks to become the chief of naval operations. James R. Schlesinger, Harold Brown, and William Cohen served as secretaries of defense during the Vietnam War and in the postwar years.

It is estimated today that there are 30,000 Jews on active duty in the US Armed Forces—about 2 percent of the total in uniform and commensurate with the total population. Jewish cadets and midshipmen also make up about 2 percent of military academy ranks. At least fifty Jews have died in the current Global War on Terrorism.

Over the 350 years of US military service by Jews, their contributions have often been downplayed, overlooked, or misrepresented. Jews in uniform have at times faced covert and overt prejudices and anti-Semitism. The most open act of anti-Semitism by a military officer came during the Civil War. On December 17, 1862, Gen. Ulysses S. Grant issued General Order No. 11 (1862), which ordered the expulsion of all Jewish civilians in his military district comprising areas of Kentucky, Tennessee, and Mississippi. Grant took the action as a means of limiting the black marketing of Southern cotton to overseas markets, which he thought was being operated "mostly by Jews and other unprincipled traders."

General Order No. 11 (1862) was short-lived. Members of the Jewish community, the US Congress, and the press made such an outcry that Pres. Abraham Lincoln rescinded the order less than a month later on January 4, 1863. While campaigning for the presidency in 1868, Grant claimed that he had no prejudice against the Jews when he issued the order; he said it was an attempt to address a problem that "certain Jews had caused."

A common and lingering misconception is that Jews have not served in any great numbers in the military. While this is false, as shown in the previous paragraphs, some well-known Americans have exploited and exaggerated this misinformation. One such person was famed writer Mark Twain. In an 1898 *Harper's* magazine article, Twain opined on how the Habsburg Empire used hatred of the Jews to help maintain national unity. Few readers in the United States had problems with that analysis, but they did not accept Twain's conclusion about American Jews. Twain wrote, "He is a frequent and faithful and capable officer in the civil service, but he is charged with an unpatriotic disinclination to stand by the flag as a soldier—like the Christian Quaker."

Twain received both support and criticism for his article. A letter to the *Harper's* editor from a Jewish lawyer said, "Tell me, therefore, from your vantage-point of cold view, what in your mind is the cause. Can American Jews do anything to correct it either in America or abroad? Will it ever come to an end? Will a Jew be permitted to live honestly, decently, and peaceably like the rest of mankind? What has become of the golden rule?"

Twain was a fine one to criticize any Jewish military stance since he had enlisted in the Confederate army early in the Civil War only to desert two weeks later to head west. When confronted with the actual numbers of Jews who had fought and died for the United States in the Civil War and other wars, Twain issued a retraction and an apology. In his article in the September 1899 issue of *Harper's*, Twain offered praise for the Jews overall:

The Jews constitute but 1% of the human race . . . It suggests a nebulous dim puff of star dust lost in the blaze of the Milky Way. Properly the Jew ought hardly be heard of; but he is heard of, has always been heard of . . . His contributions to the world's list of great names are away out of proportion to the weakness of his numbers. He has made a marvelous fight in the world, in all the ages; and has done it with his hands tied behind him. He could be vain of himself, and be excused for it. The Egyptian, the Babylonian, and the Persian rose . . . the Greek and the Roman followed, and made a vast noise, and they are gone . . . The Jew saw them all, and is now what he always was, exhibiting no decadence, no infirmities of age, no dulling of his alert mind. All things are mortal but the Jew . . . What is the secret of his immortality?

To counter misconceptions such as Twain's and to recognize and preserve the history of Jews in the American military, former uniformed personnel formed the Jewish War Veterans of the United States of America in 1896. The organization, the oldest veterans group in the United States, described its purposes in its National Constitution preamble:

To maintain true allegiance to the United States of America; to foster and perpetuate true Americanism; to combat whatever tends to impair the efficiency and permanency of our free institutions; to uphold the fair name of the Jew and fight his or her battles wherever unjustly assailed; to encourage the doctrine of universal liberty, equal rights, and full justice to all men and women; to combat the powers of bigotry darkness wherever originating and whatever their target; to preserve the spirit of comradeship by mutual helpfulness to comrades and their families; to cooperate with and support existing educational institutions and establish educational institutions, and to foster the education of ex-servicemen and ex-servicewomen, and our members in the ideals and principles of Americanism; to instill love of country and flag, and to promote sound minds and bodies in our members and our youth; to preserve the memories and records of patriotic service performed by the men and women of our faith; to honor their memory and shield from neglect the graves of our heroic dead.

The Jewish War Veterans established the National Museum of American Jewish Military History in Washington, DC, in 1958. Its stated purpose is to document and preserve "the contributions of Jewish Americans to the peace and freedom of the United States . . . and to educate the public concerning the courage, heroism, and sacrifices made by Jewish Americans who served in the Armed Forces."

The museum honors all Jews who have served in uniform. It has special displays dedicated to Medal of Honor recipients, but its officials do not enter the debate about who is and who is not a Jew. As for the religion of individual recipients, the museum's policy is to follow and accept the findings and decisions of the Congressional Medal of Honor Society.

The Medal of Honor

THE MEDAL OF HONOR is the highest award for bravery given by the US Armed Forces for combat against an enemy force. It is awarded to those who distinguish themselves by gallantry and intrepidity beyond the call of duty at the risk of their own lives. Generally presented by the president in the name of Congress and often called the Congressional Medal of Honor, the award has been bestowed on only 3,500 service members of the more than 40 million men and women who have served in US forces since the formation of the Continental Army in 1775. At least seventeen of the recipients are Jewish.

Armed forces around the world have always recognized and rewarded acts of bravery. Decorations for distinguished service not only spotlighted the brave but also served as an incentive for more such valor. French emperor Napoleon Bonaparte said, "Give me enough medals and I'll win you any war." He added, "A soldier will fight long and hard for a bit of colored ribbon."

The first effort to recognize valor on the part of Americans came from Gen. George Washington when he established the Badge of Military Merit on August 7, 1782. Intended to be granted for "any singularly meritorious action," it was awarded to only three persons before it fell into disuse after the conclusion of the American Revolution. The original Badge of Military Merit was a heart-shaped piece of purple cloth with an embroidered "Merit" on the face. It was revived in 1932 as the Purple Heart to be awarded to wounded veterans of World War I.

For the next fifty years the US military had no formal way of recognizing valor on the battlefield. The expansion of the army in the Mexican American

War (1846–1848) brought new demands for honoring the brave. On March 23, 1847, the US Congress authorized the Certificate of Merit "to any private soldier who had distinguished himself by gallantry performed in the presence of the enemy." The certificates were discontinued after the war but then reintroduced in 1876 after the Battle of the Little Bighorn.

The mass mobilization, huge battles, and general carnage of the American Civil War brought the need for creating a new medal for valor. When Congress and the military took up discussions, there were objections that such an award was "too European;" smacked of Old World vanity, elitism, and snobbery; and had no place in democratic America. However, the majority agreed that it was time for a national medal to recognize military bravery. On December 9, 1861, Sen. James W. Grimes of Iowa introduced a bill that authorized the distribution of "medals of honor" to be awarded to sailors and marines who distinguished themselves in battle. Sen. Henry Wilson of Massachusetts introduced a similar bill on February 17, 1862, authorizing the Medal of Honor to be awarded to army personnel. Pres. Abraham Lincoln signed both bills, and the most prominent and honored military medal became a permanent part of United States history.

Although initially authorized only for Civil War heroes, the Medal of Honor was made permanent by Congress on March 3, 1863. The legislation also extended eligibility to officers in addition to enlisted personnel. It placed no restrictions on when a medal could be approved, and applications continued for decades after the war concluded. Because there were no specific criteria or time limits for awarding the medal, it was liberally presented—some to individuals and even entire units who had performed few acts of bravery or none.

In 1876 a new standard for eligibility for the Medal of Honor stated, "The [individual's] conduct which deserves such recognition should not be the simple discharge of duty, but such acts beyond this if omitted or refused to be done, should not justly subject the person to censure as a shortcoming or failure."

The US Congress passed legislation in 1897 specifying that the Medal of Honor could only be awarded for "gallantry and intrepidity." In 1905, Pres. Theodore Roosevelt, by executive order, outlined the basic policy and procedures for awarding the medal. The order stated that, whenever possible, award ceremonies would be held in Washington, DC, with the president or his designated representative making the presentation.

On January 11, 1905, the Certificate of Merit was changed to the Certificate of Merit Medal. This remained until World War I when the Merit Medal was replaced by the Army Distinguished Service Medal on January 2, 1918, and the Navy Distinguished Service Medal the following year. The 1918 act also authorized the Distinguished Service Cross and the Navy Cross for valor on the battlefield that did not merit a Medal of Honor as well as the Citation Star, which was replaced by the Silver Star in 1932.

Later, in 1916, Congress established the Medal of Honor Review Board "for the purpose of investigating and reporting upon past awards or issue of the so-called Congressional Medal of Honor by or through the War Department; this with a view to ascertain what Medals of Honor, if any, had been awarded or issued for any cause other than distinguished conduct by an officer or enlisted man in action involving actual conflict with an enemy."

A panel of five former generals was formed to review each of the 2,625 recipients who had been honored since the medal's creation, including 1,520 Civil War recipients; 443 Indian Wars recipients; and 662 Spanish-American War recipients. The board's final report, which came out in 1917, removed 911 names from the list of Medal of Honor recipients. Most of the deleted were from Civil War abuses of the award, such as whole regiments that had received the medal for extending their enlistment dates. Six civilians deemed not eligible for the military award were also eliminated.

While there is only one award called the Medal of Honor, as such, there are three different service renditions: the Army Medal of Honor, the Navy Medal of Honor, and the Air Force Medal of Honor. The US Coast Guard, organized in 1915, serves as part of the navy in wartime, and its members are eligible for the Navy Medal of Honor. One member has been so honored. Marines also receive the Navy Medal of Honor. The US Air Force, formerly part of the Army Air Corps and established as a separate service in 1947, continued to award the army version of the Medal of Honor until Congress authorized the Air Force Medal of Honor in 1956.

In 1944 a light blue moiré neck ribbon was added to display the medal. The center of the ribbon displays thirteen white stars in the form of three chevrons. Both the top and middle chevrons are made up of five stars, with the bottom chevron made of three stars.

On July 25, 1963, the US Congress amended previous Medal of Honor legislation to read that the medal is to be awarded to those who distinguish themselves . . .

conspicuously by gallantry and intrepidity at the risk of his life above and beyond the call of duty while engaged in an action against an enemy of the United States; while engaged in military operations involving conflict with an opposing foreign force; or while serving with friendly foreign forces engaged in an armed conflict against an opposing armed force in which the United States is not a belligerent party. The deed performed must have been one of personal bravery or self-sacrifice so conspicuous as to clearly distinguish the individual above his comrades and must have involved risk of life. Incontestable proof of the performance of the service will be exacted and each recommendation for the award of this decoration will be considered on the standard of extraordinary merit.

Since the 1980s, a few Medals of Honor for actions dating all the way back to the Civil War have been awarded to correct past oversights and administrative errors. In 2002 the Department of Defense began a congressionally mandated review of decorations from World War II, Korea, and Vietnam. The records of African American, Asian American, Jewish American, and Hispanic American Distinguished Service Cross recipients were reviewed to see if racial discrimination had denied them their country's highest medal for valor. As a result, in 2014 the Medal of Honor was awarded to twenty-four additional recipients.

Designs of the Medals of Honor have changed over the years but still closely resemble those of the original Civil War awards. The Institute of Heraldry, as authorized by Public Law 85-263, approved in September 1957, delineates the authority of the secretary of the army to furnish heraldic services to the military departments and other branches of the federal government. It describes the Army Medal of Honor as "a five pointed star, each point tipped with trefoils, 1½ inches wide, surrounded by a green laurel wreath and suspended from a gold bar inscribed *VALOR*, surmounted by an eagle. In the center of the star, Minerva's (the Roman goddess of war) head is surrounded by the words *UNITED STATES OF AMERICA*. On each ray of the star is a green oak leaf. On the reverse is a bar engraved *THE CONGRESS TO* with a space for engraving the name of the recipient." The pendant and suspension bar are made of gilding metal, with the eye, jump rings, and suspension ring made of red brass. The finish on the pendant and suspension bar is hard enameled, gold-plated, and rose gold–plated, with polished highlights. It is suspended from an eagle holding cannons and cannonballs in its talons.

The Institute describes the Navy Medal of Honor as "a five-pointed bronze star, tipped with trefoils containing a crown of laurel and oak. In the center is Minerva, personifying the United States, standing with left hand resting on fasces and right hand holding a shield blazoned with the shield from the coat of arms of the United States. She repulses Discord, represented by snakes. The medal is suspended from the flukes of an anchor." It is made of solid red brass, oxidized and buffed.

According to the institute, the Air Force Medal of Honor is "within a wreath of green laurel, a gold five-pointed star, one point down, tipped with trefoils and each point containing a crown of laurel and oak on a green background. Centered on the star, an annulet of 34 stars is a representation of the head of the Statue of Liberty. The star is suspended from a bar inscribed with the word *VALOR* above an adaptation of the thunderbolt from the Air Force Coat of Arms." The pendant is made of gilding metal. The connecting bar, hinge, and pin are made of bronze. The finish on the pendant and suspension bar is hard enameled, gold-plated, and rose gold–plated, with buffed relief.

Compensation, privileges, and courtesies are extended to those who receive the Medal of Honor. Currently, recipients receive a pension of $1,406.72 per month, as of 2020, which is subject to cost-of-living increases. Retired recipients receive a 10 percent increase in their retirement pay. Recipients also receive a Medal of Honor Flag, the privilege to wear the uniform anytime as long as the standard restrictions are observed, authorization for burial in Arlington National Cemetery in Washington, DC, and admission of their qualified children to the US military academies without nomination and quota requirements. Although not required by law or military regulation, recipients receive recognition salutes from members of the armed forces as a form of respect and courtesy regardless of rank or status.

Recipients of the Medal of Honor are also recognized in the Hall of Heroes in the Pentagon in Washington, DC. Three versions of the Medal of Honor—Army, Air Force, and Sea Service (Navy, Marine Corps, and Coast Guard)—are displayed in the hall along with the names of the recipients. On May 14, 1968, Pres. Lyndon B. Johnson awarded the Medal of Honor to four servicemen in a Pentagon Center Courtyard ceremony. Following the ceremony, he ascended a staircase to the Pentagon's A Ring's second floor overlooking the courtyard and cut a ribbon to the entrance to the Hall of Heroes. During the Pentagon renovation of the 1990s the hall was moved to its current location on the main concourse. Today it is used for promotion, retirement, and other types of award ceremonies.

In a speech on June 22, 2000, US Army Chief of Staff Gen. Eric S. Shinseki spoke at an induction ceremony of recent recipients of the Medal of Honor into the Pentagon Hall of Heroes. He said then what has remained true about the men who have received the award since its authorization more than a century and a half ago. General Shinseki said, "The Medal of Honor is not something soldiers seek. No one can train for it. In fact, no one expects people to make the kinds of sacrifice required in order to receive it."

PART 1

Jewish Medal of Honor Recipients

★★★

1

Benjamin B. Levy,
Civil War, US Army

Company G, 1st New York Volunteer Infantry Regiment

Glendale, Virginia, June 30, 1862

Date Presented: March 1, 1865

CITATION:
This soldier, a drummer boy, took the gun of a sick comrade, went into the fight, and when the color bearers were shot down, carried the colors and saved them from capture.

BENJAMIN LEVY was the first and youngest Jewish American to earn the Medal of Honor. He was born on February 22, 1845, in New York City to Robert and Pauline Levy, who had recently immigrated to the United States from Germany. Both of his parents held strong abolitionist views.

At the outbreak of the Civil War, volunteers in New York City enlisted for two years and formed the 1st New York Volunteer Infantry Regiment on Staten Island in late April and early May of 1861. On May 26 the regiment embarked for Fortress Monroe, Virginia, and participated in the Battle of Big Bethel on June 10. After the fight, the 1st New York returned to Fortress Monroe before taking up positions in Newport News on July 3 where it remained for nearly a year.

During the winter of 1861–1862, the 1st New York received 320 recruits. Among them was Benjamin Levy, who volunteered on October 21, 1861. Because he was only sixteen years of age, he was assigned as a musician (drummer) rather than as an infantryman. Drummers were considered noncombatants as they were armed with nothing but their drum and sticks. They played an important role, however, beyond maintaining a beat for parades and ceremonies. In battle the drummers played dozens of different drum calls to communicate orders from commanders to their soldiers. During and after battles, drummers helped evacuate the wounded and assisted in the field hospitals. Levy's younger brother Robert, fourteen, volunteered about this same time and served as drummer in the 7th New York Volunteer Infantry Regiment.

In camp, drummers performed whatever task their commander desired. Soon after Levy's arrival at Newport News, he assumed the additional duty of courier and orderly for his brigade commander, Gen. Joseph K. Mansfield. One of his duties was to carry messages from Mansfield to his superior and Department of Virginia commander Gen. John E. Wool. During one of these courier missions, Levy boarded the steamer *Express* with his message pouch to deliver it to Wool's headquarters at Fortress Monroe. His fellow passengers included several officers and two paymasters. The steamer also towed a water schooner for delivery to warships at anchor off the fort.

Soon after the *Express* began its voyage through Hampton Roads and into Chesapeake Bay, the Confederate gunboat *Sea Bird* spotted it and gave chase. The *Express* was in imminent danger of capture or sinking when Levy raced to the stern of the ship and, with his knife that had been a gift from his mother, cut the tow rope to the water schooner. With the reduced drag, the *Express* easily outdistanced the *Sea Bird* and made its way to the protection of the guns of Fortress Monroe and the anchored Union warships.

The ship's crew and passengers praised Levy for his quick action. Generals Mansfield and Wool commended the New York drummer boy with a "mention in the dispatches."

In June 1862 the Union army, under the command of Gen. George B. McClellan, began its offensive to capture the Confederate capital of Richmond in what became known as the Seven Days' Battles of the Peninsula Campaign. McClellan made it to the point where he "could see the church spires of Richmond" before the Army of Virginia, commanded by Gen. Robert E. Lee, counterattacked. The Union army soon was in full retreat back down the peninsula.

General Mansfield requested that Levy remain as his orderly when the 1st New York deployed to act as rear guard during the first days of the campaign. Levy respectively turned down the request in order to return to his regiment as its drummer. The 1st New York did not become actively engaged until the Battle of the Peach Orchard on June 29, when it covered the Union's retreat against Confederate sharpshooters and guerillas.

That evening of the 29th, Levy commandeered the rifle and cartilage belt of a fellow soldier suffering from malaria after he discarded his drum, which either he had purposefully broken or enemy fire had damaged. During the afternoon of June 30, the Confederate main force caught up with the retreating Union army at Glendale, also known as the Battle of Frayser's Farm.

All but two of the regiment's four color-bearer sergeants and the four corporals who accompanied them fell early in the battle, causing the ranks of the 1st New York to run to the rear. Levy rushed forward and took the colors from a wounded sergeant. As he waved the colors to rally the regiment, another color-bearer beside him was wounded. Levy discarded his borrowed rifle and, with colors in each hand, helped organize an orderly retreat despite a slight wound.

As Levy broke out of a tree line carrying the two colors, Gen. Philip Kearney, commander of the sector, observed Levy's courage and promoted him on the spot to color sergeant. Kearney and other officers later recommended Levy for the Medal of Honor for his actions.

From Glendale, the 1st New York fell back to Malvern Hill. During the march, their uniforms became so covered in dust that a Union artillery battery mistook them for the enemy and opened fire. Col. Garrett Dyckman ordered Levy into an open area to wave the colors to identify their unit. Levy did so and the firing ceased, but Confederate sharpshooters in nearby woods fired at the color sergeant. Bullets struck the colors staff as well as a tin cup on Levy's haversack. He fell to the ground, tied his colors up with his handkerchief, and rolled over and over back to his regiment's lines, successfully arriving to the cheers and laughter of his fellow soldiers.

Levy and the 1st New York fought at the Second Battle of Manassas on August 28–30, at Chantilly on September 1, and at Fredericksburg on December 13 before going into winter quarters at Falmouth on the north bank of the Rappahannock River. On May 1–5, 1863, they were engaged in the Battle of Chancellorsville. After the fight they embarked at Aquia Creek bound for Washington, DC, from where they traveled to New York City to be mustered out upon completion of their two-year enlistment. On May 10, the city honored the veterans with a reception and dinner; the regiment was formally mustered out on May 25. During its two years of service, the 1st New York

Regiment suffered 226 deaths—113 in actual battles, 79 from wounds, and 34 from accidents and disease.

Levy did not remain a civilian for long. In January 1864 he enlisted as a private in the 40th New York Volunteer Infantry Regiment, a unit that had been formed in during June 1861 and had fought in most of the battles in the East. Called the "Mozart Regiment" in recognition of the recruitment assistance provided by the Mozart Hall Committee—a New York City political group—the 40th New York was heralded for its performance on the battlefield as a combat unit, eclipsed only by the famed 69th New York Regiment—the "Irish Brigade."

It is likely that Levy knew many of the members of the 40th New York from his time before the war in New York City and the period when the 1st New York and the 40th New York shared quarters in Falmouth in the winter of 1862–1863. Even so, Levy's service in the 40th was to be brief. On May 5, 1864, he was seriously wounded in the Battle of the Wilderness. Evacuated to a field hospital, Levy and other patients—along with their doctors—were captured the next day by partisans of the 35th Virginia Cavalry Battalion, led by Lt. Col. Elijah White. Levy lay in the open with little protection from the elements or care for his wound for two weeks before a unit of "colored troops" from Fredericksburg retook the field hospital.

He was hospitalized for more than a year at the Mount Pleasant Hospital in Washington, DC, and then at the Broad and Cherry Street Hospital in Philadelphia. On May 31, 1865, he was medically discharged with this explanation: "Sequence of gun-shot wound, middle third left thigh; received at the Battle of the Wilderness, Va., May 5, 1864. The thigh bone was fractured, wound was subsequently attacked with gangrene; two inches shortening; patient can endure little or no fatigue; degree of disability one-half."

Given the fog of war and the restricted communication systems of the time, commanders were not always certain about the hows and whys of awarding Medals of Honor once the award had been authorized. As a result of both combat disorder and administrative snafus, many medals were not awarded until years after the conflict concluded. This was not the case with Levy. The actions that earned him the medal were both decisive and observed by his sector commander, ensuring that Levy, the first Jewish recipient, was recognized for his bravery in a timely fashion and in an appropriate manner. Unlike many postwar-approved medals that were delivered unceremoniously to the worthy veteran by the US Postal Service, Gen. Ulysses S. Grant personally pinned Levy's metal on his chest on March 1, 1865, shortly before his discharge from the hospital.

Levy returned to New York City after his discharge, where he went to work in the Customs House as a clerk. He married Olive Angele Perkins, daughter of Joseph A. and Salome Wallace Perkins, both born in the United States, on June 21, 1865, at the New York City Methodist Episcopal Church. Over the next seventeen years, they had six children. Olive died on October 14, 1907, at their home on 167 West 143rd Street in Manhattan and is buried in Cypress Hills Cemetery in Brooklyn. Levy later married Matilda C. Schroeder, widow of John Schroeder. Matilda died on March 3, 1920.

In addition to his work at the Custom House, Levy remained active in civic organizations and Grand Army of the Republic activities. He was a member of Emanuel Lodge No. 654, Free and Accepted Masons (F. & A. M). He also served as the adjutant of the headquarters of the Army and Navy Medal of Honor Legion of the United States of America.

On July 20, 1921, Levy died of heart disease at age seventy-six at his home at 301 West 150th Street in Manhattan. He is buried in Cypress Hills Cemetery, next to his first wife, Olive, and a daughter who died in 1888. Levy's younger brother Robert survived him and made the death notification to the US Pension Office.

A Virginia State Historical Marker in Glendale identifies the location where Levy earned his Medal of Honor. On May 27, 2001, a ceremony was held to mark the replacement Medal of Honor headstone, complete with a Star of David, for Levy at Cypress Hills Cemetery.

Gen. Daniel E. Sickles, a fellow New Yorker and Medal of Honor recipient himself, was one of Levy's commanders during the Peninsula Campaign. He wrote shortly after the end of the war, "Levy was a soldier of remarkable merit and was highly esteemed and noticed for gallantry and good conduct by Generals Phil Kearney, Mansfield, Birney, Berry, and Egan. He also served under my command, and I am glad to testify as a soldier, to his bravery and gallantry."

★★★

2

Abraham Cohn,
Civil War, US Army

6th New Hampshire Volunteer Infantry

Wilderness, Virginia, May 6, 1864, and Petersburg, Virginia, July 30, 1864

Date Presented: August 24, 1865

CITATION:

*During Battle of the Wilderness on May 6, 1864, rallied and formed,
under heavy fire, disorganized and fleeing troops of different regiments.
At Petersburg, Va., July 30, 1864, bravely and coolly carried orders to
the advanced line under severe fire.*

ABRAHAM COHN earned his Medal of Honor for valor displayed in two of
the most intense battles of the Civil War. Born on June 17, 1832, at Guttentag,
Silesia, in East Prussia, to Nathan Cohn, who was the mayor of the village, the
future soldier attended local schools before entering the University of Berlin.
There he studied medicine and underwent basic military training before he
left to become a schoolteacher.

In 1860, at the age of twenty-eight, Cohn joined the flood of German Jews
who immigrated to the United States to escape anti-Semitism in Europe and
for better opportunities in the Western Hemisphere. At the outbreak of the
Civil War, he volunteered for a three-year enlistment at New York City in the
68th New York Volunteer Infantry Regiment on July 22, 1861. Cohn (some of
the official documents misspell his name as Kohn), a fairly small man even by
the standard of the mid-nineteenth century, was described in his enlistment
papers as a teacher of five feet five and a half inches in height with a florid

complexion, blue eyes, and black hair. Because of his prior military training in Berlin, Cohn was mustered in as a sergeant in the regiment's Company B on August 1 and rapidly advanced in rank. On January 14, 1862, he was commissioned a 2nd lieutenant in Company K and then on April 30 was promoted to 1st lieutenant and transferred to Company A. Cohn was promoted to captain in Company E on October 17.

The 68th New York, composed mostly of German-born immigrants primarily from New York—with some volunteers from Pennsylvania, Maryland, and New Jersey—and often referred to as the "German Rifles," initially served in the defense of Washington, DC. Other than a few light skirmishes with Confederate patrols, Cohn and his regiment saw little combat during his first year.

On December 17, 1862, Cohn was "discharged for disability" after he contacted an unknown illness. He settled in Campton, New Hampshire, where he sufficiently recovered to again volunteer for the Union army. On January 5, 1864, Cohn joined Company E, 6th New Hampshire Volunteer Infantry Regiment, as a private. During the next year, he rose in rank and was promoted to sergeant major on March 28, 1864. He then became a 1st lieutenant in Company C on July 17, 1865, and assumed the position of regimental adjutant on the following March 15. During his sixteen months' service with the 6th New Hampshire, Cohn participated in eleven battles and was twice wounded.

In May 1864, Abraham Cohn, while still a sergeant major, and the 6th New Hampshire Regiment were in the midst of the Battle of the Wilderness, so named for the nearby small town surrounded by thick forest and dense underbrush. This is where Generals Ulysses S. Grant and Robert E. Lee met in combat for the first time. On May 5 the two armies engaged in heavy fighting with neither gaining an advantage. By nightfall, both forces had withdrawn and built log and earthen defenses.

Early the next morning Grant's army attacked the Confederate right and left flanks, forcing the rebels into retreat. Just as it appeared the Union force would win the day, Confederate reinforcements under the command of Gen. James Longstreet arrived, stopped the advance, and then began to drive the Union forces back. When Union soldiers all along the line began to withdraw in an unorderly run, Cohn exposed himself to halt his troops as well as those of other units. According to his Medal of Honor citation, he displayed "conspicuous gallantry in rallying and forming under heavy fire disorganized and fleeing troops of different regiments." His actions and those of other Union leaders stabilized the lines. By nightfall the two armies basically occupied the same breastworks as the previous evening.

The New Hampshire soldier was not the only Jewish American to earn the Medal of Honor on that day in the Wilderness clash. Along the same battle line, Leopold Karpeles of the 56th Massachusetts Infantry Regiment performed a similar valorous act and was later awarded the medal.

Later in May, Cohn and the 6th New Hampshire served in the battles of Spotsylvania Court House and North Anna River. Then they fought at Cold Harbor in June and in the middle of the month joined the siege of Lee's army at Petersburg. On July 30 the Union forces exploded a large amount of explosives in a tunnel dug beneath the Confederate lines. Union forces poured into the breach of the rebel defenses, only to meet stiff resistance from reinforcements. During the battle Cohn, despite suffering a shoulder wound, took on the role of messenger as, according to his citation, he "bravely and coolly carried orders to the advanced line under severe fire."

Cohn served for the remainder of the Petersburg Campaign. He was wounded in the final attack on Petersburg on April 2. While there is no complete remaining documentation, Cohn apparently recovered sufficiently to participate in the pursuit of Lee's army in the Appomattox Campaign. In late April the 6th New Hampshire transferred to Washington, DC, where the regiment marched in the Grand Review of the Armies victory parade on May 23.

On July 17, 1865, Cohn mustered out of the army. Ten days later the remainder of the 6th New Hampshire was disbanded. During its service in the Civil War, the regiment had an authorized strength of a little more than 600. It lost a total of 10 officers, and 177 enlisted men were killed or mortally wounded. An additional 3 officers and 228 enlisted men died of disease for a total of 418 deaths.

Cohn had settled back in New York and was residing at 439 8th Avenue when his Medal of Honor for the two battles was awarded on August 14, 1865. On August 17, the adjutant general of New Hampshire, Natt Head, later governor of the state, issued a letter "To Whom It May Concern." Head wrote, "I take great pleasure in bearing the testimony of the faithful service of Adjutant Abraham Cohn, both as a private and as an officer in the late 6th Regiment of New Hampshire Volunteer Infantry. His record in connection with this regiment has been one of great fidelity and ability and his successive promotions have been well merited rewards. I am also happy to bear testimony to the untiring industry and literary ability which Adjutant Cohn has displayed in collecting data for an official history of the Sixth Regiment, New Hampshire Volunteer Infantry."

Bvt. Maj. Gen. S. G. Griffin, US Volunteers, also penned a letter from his home in Keene, New Hampshire, on November 23, 1865, praising Cohn. Griffin, the future Speaker of the House of Representatives of New Hampshire, wrote, "This certifies that Abraham Cohn enlisted in the 6th Volunteers, of which regiment I was the Colonel, on the 5th day of January, 1864. He at once attracted the attention and won the approbation of his officers by his soldierly bearing and faithful performance of duty, as well as by his accomplishments in being able to communicate with recruits from European countries in their own various languages."

The general continued, "On the 28th day of March 1864, he was promoted to the position of Sergeant Major of the regiment, and throughout the great campaign that followed—from the Rapidan to the capture of Petersburg and Richmond—displayed remarkable bravery and coolness in action, endurance in the field and efficiency in his office. He was wounded at the 'Battle of the Mine' in front of Petersburg, July 30, 1864, where he won a 'Medal of Honor' for his distinguished bravery awarded by the War Department."

Griffin concluded, "In appreciation of his meritorious services during this campaign he was promoted to the rank of Adjutant of his regiment, in which capacity he remained until the close of the war, winning the esteem and admiration of all who knew him by his gentlemanly and officer-like deportment, his sobriety and integrity, and by his noble devotion to the cause of the country of his adoption."

Cohn became a successful businessman and merchant in New York City and on June 18, 1867, married Fanny (recorded as Francis in some documents) Zeller, an immigrant from Berlin, Germany, in New York's Temple Beth El Abraham. Cohn was thirty-five years of age at the time, Fanny twenty-one. The 1870 federal census, dated June 22, lists the Cohns and their two children as residents of New York City's Ward 16, District 12. Over the following years, Abraham and Fanny added six more children to their family.

Little is known about the Cohns over the next two decades other than that he applied for and received a passport on November 11, 1876. There is no record of Cohn's travels outside the United States, but he likely used the passport to return to Germany to visit family. Another brief record notes that

Cohn's continued receipt of a pension of $16 per month was reconfirmed on April 18, 1894.

During his final years, Cohn and his family lived at 36 East 84th Street in New York City. He died at the city's German Hospital after a prolonged illness of three years on June 2, 1897, just two weeks before his sixty-fifth birthday. His death certificate notes the cause of death as heart failure contributed by pneumonia and the place of burial as Cypress Hills Cemetery.

The *New York Times* published his obituary on June 5 and included a summary of the actions that led to his receipt of the Medal of Honor. It also stated that after the war he "engaged in business and accumulated a fortune." It concluded that he was to be buried in the nonsectarian Cypress Hills Cemetery in Brooklyn.

For nearly a century thereafter, the death certificate and newspaper claim that Cohn was buried in Cypress Hills Cemetery was accepted as the truth and included in every biography and article about the Civil War hero. No one questioned just why a proud Jew would be buried in a nonsectarian graveyard until the 1980s, when researchers began efforts to document and photograph the gravesite of each recipient of the Medal of Honor. Queries to the New Hampshire Bureau of Vital Records and Statistics resulted in the previously mentioned information about Cypress Hills Cemetery, but subsequent correspondence revealed that the cemetery had no record of Cohn. Researchers surmised at the time that the location of the grave had been "lost."

In 2010 later researchers found sources that claimed Cohn had been buried in the backyard of his family home and that the Cypress Hills Cemetery name had been used for respectability. He had been later disinterred and moved to an unknown site. Still others refuted these claims and insisted he was buried in Cypress Hills.

Finally in the second decade of the twenty-first century, after research in nearly every Jewish burial ground in the New York City area, Abraham Cohn's final resting place was discovered in Section 15, Lot 2, of the Beth Olam Cemetery in Ridgewood, Queens. His wife Fanny, who died on April 21, 1928, is buried at his side. The Beth Olam Cemetery, established in 1851, provides free burial plots for members of Congregation Shearith Israel.

The reasons for the inaccurate information and confusion may be simple. The address for the Beth Olam Cemetery is 2 Cypress Hills Street. The doctor who completed Cohn's death certificate likely recorded Cypress Hills Cemetery by mistake. The reporter for the *New York Times* took his information from the death certificate. Another explanation is that both the Cypress Hills and Beth Olam cemeteries are in an area generally referred to as Cypress Hills. Some funeral directors as well as doctors who signed death certificates referred to the entire area as "Cypress Hills" on occasion.

While Cohn's gravesite may have been lost for nearly a century, the location of his Medal of Honor is well documented. It is preserved in the collection of the National Museum of American Jewish Military History in Washington, DC.

★★★

3

Leopold Karpeles,
Civil War, US Army

Company E, 57th Massachusetts Volunteer Infantry

Wilderness, Virginia, May 6, 1864

Date Presented: April 30, 1870

CITATION:
*While color bearer, rallied the retreating troops and induced
them to check the enemy's advance.*

LEOPOLD KARPELES emigrated from Europe to the United States and
earned one of the first Medals of Honor of the Civil War. He did not, however,
receive the award until a half decade after the conflict concluded. Born on
September 9, 1838, to Joachim, a successful cloth manufacturer, and Susanna
Karpeles in Prague, Bohemia (current Czech Republic), Leopold and his older
brother Emil attended Catholic schools, an arrangement for Jews not unusual
in Prague at the time.

During his early youth, Karpeles often vacationed outside Prague with
his parents on farms and resorts owned by relatives, where he learned to ride
horses and developed an affection for the outdoors. This would come in handy
when at age eleven he sailed for America to join his brother Emil, who had
immigrated earlier to the Texas Gulf Coast. In Galveston the younger Karpeles worked as a helper and clerk in his brother's general merchandise store.
In his late teens and early twenties, Karpeles led supply caravans to and from
Mexico. Family members later mentioned that he served with a paramilitary
unit known as the Brownsville Guards or the Brownsville Militia in fights

against border bandits and hostile Native Americans. Brownsville historians confirm that there was a militia unit known as the Brownsville Rifles, formed during this period to fight the bandit and revolutionary leader Juan Cortina, but Karpeles is not on its muster roll. It is likely that Karpeles and his caravan, passing through Brownsville, united with the Rifles for self-protection on their trade expeditions into Mexico. Some sources also state that Karpeles served as "the youngest member of the Texas Rangers," but this claim is not supported by documents in the Texas Ranger Hall of Fame and Museum. Again, he may very well have informally joined the Rangers in their defense of the frontier.

As he grew older, Karpeles differed more and more with his brother on the issues of religion and slavery. Emil had been impressed with the Catholics while in school in Prague and became a supporter of the church in Galveston. He became such a staunch Catholic that he helped fund the building for the Ursuline Convent and, when he died, left his entire fortune to the nuns. Emil also accepted the Southern system of slavery while Leopold remained true to his Jewish heritage and devoted abolitionism.

In 1861, Karpeles, with his brother's encouragement, departed Galveston for Massachusetts. Part of the reason for this move was for a business opportunity, but mostly it was because of his continued opposition to slavery and the possibility of secession by Texas from the Union. His great-granddaughter later wrote that Karpeles "had seen and abhorred slavery" and settled in Massachusetts because it was the center of the abolitionist movement.

In Springfield, Karpeles, as one of the city's first Jewish residents, found employment as a clerk in a general store. He made friends with Samuel B. Spooner and met many of the state's abolition leaders, was involved in the Underground Railroad, which assisted runaway slaves, and became a great admirer of Pres. Abraham Lincoln.

On August 15, 1862, Karpeles enlisted as a private in Company A of the 46th Massachusetts Volunteer Infantry Regiment, commanded by his friend Spooner. During its ten months of active duty, the 46th Massachusetts fielded 43 officers and 954 enlisted men and saw action in several minor battles in North Carolina. Of these, one died in battle while another thirty-two succumbed to accidents or disease before the regiment mustered out upon completion of its enlistment.

Karpeles's official military records describe him as five feet five inches tall, with a dark complexion and black eyes and hair. During his ten-month enlistment, Karpeles advanced in rank to corporal and color-bearer before his honorable discharge on July 29, 1863. In a letter of recommendation on May 17, 1864, his company commander Spooner wrote, "This is to certify that Leopold Karpeles is a corporal of Company A of this regiment. In the battles of Kingston, Whitehall, and Goldsborough he bore the State colors. The promptness with which he came upon the line of battle and the firmness with which he stood his ground, though the flag was several times pierced by the bullets of the enemy, were so conspicuous as to be the subject of remark and commendation. I have no hesitation in endorsing him as a man who in any position would only have to know his duty, and he would discharge it to the best of his ability."

Col. W. S. Shurtless, commander of the 46th Regiment, wrote, "I very readily give my testimony to the efficiency and soldierly qualities of Leopold Karpeles, having frequently remarked and observed his alertness, promptness, and faithfulness to duty."

Karpeles returned to work as a clerk in a general store after his discharge, but his time in uniform had made such an impression that he spent his off hours writing about his experiences. He wrote, "I marched in an inspired manner with my flag waving proudly for all to see and cheer. I am aware that while I'm providing a rallying point and courage for my comrades, I'm also a prime target for the enemy. I vowed to accept that risk when I assumed this obligation which I consider a privilege and honor. My dedication to my country's flag rests on my ardent belief in this noblest of causes, equality for all. If my future rests under this earth rather than upon it, I fear not."

Either out of the boredom of working as a clerk, or more likely from sense of adventure, Karpeles reenlisted on March 7, 1864, at Camp Wool in Worcester, Massachusetts, for a three- year tour as a private in the 57th Massachusetts Volunteer Infantry Regiment. Because of his experience, Karpeles quickly rose up the ranks with promotion to sergeant on April 14.

The 57th Regiment was in great need of veteran leaders. Its men, mostly poor Irishmen in their mid-twenties, came from eighteen states and thirteen foreign countries, but only a few had prior military experience. On April 6, 1864, the 57th was formally mustered into the army and was quickly dispatched to the Virginia battlefront. The regiment moved to Baltimore and then to Washington, D.C., where it passed in review before the corps commander, Gen. Ambrose Burnside, and President Lincoln on April 25.

After a brief encampment at Arlington, Virginia, the 57th Regiment marched toward the Rappahannock on April 27. The 57th joined the Battle of the Wilderness on its second day when Confederate forces counterattacked and threatened to overrun the Union positions. Gen. James Samuel Wadsworth, the commander of the 1st Division, to which the 57th was assigned, rode up and down the collapsing Union line in an attempt to rally the troops. When he spotted Karpeles carrying what appeared to be the only remaining Union colors on the field, Wadsworth ordered him to take a stand and shouted for the remaining soldiers to rally around the flag. To make his position more prominent, Karpeles stood on top of a tree stump in the midst of the battle to mark the division's defensive line.

Karpeles's efforts were successful in that the Union forces held. The victory came at a high price. General Wadsworth fell mortally wounded and the 57th lost 262 of its assigned 548 men. Although his flag was pierced multiple times with bullets and shrapnel, Karpeles survived the battle uninjured and was recommended for the Medal of Honor. In the same fight, fellow Jewish American Abraham Cohn also earned the Medal of Honor.

Ceremonies would have to wait, however, as regimental and higher officials were faced with far more challenges than paperwork and award documentation. Immediately after the Battle of the Wilderness, the 57th Regiment, with Karpeles still carrying its colors, joined the fight at Spotsylvania Court House on May 8–21. After the battle the Union army continued its pursuit of the retreating Confederate army and again engaged in combat at North Anna, Virginia, on May 23. Karpeles led the way, carrying the colors in the regiment's attack against the enemy breastworks. Early in the battle a bullet struck Karpeles in the knee. He continued to wave his flag as he advanced until he could no longer stand due to loss of blood.

Initially treated at his division's field hospital, Karpeles transferred through a series of hospitals in Virginia and Baltimore, Maryland, during the next year before arriving at Mount Pleasant General Hospital in Washington, DC, on February 4, 1865. According to his Army of the United States Certificate of Disability for Discharge, he was released on May 1, 1865, on "total disability" because of "partial paralysis" from his leg wound, which made him "incapable of performing the duties of a soldier."

Karpeles returned to Springfield, Massachusetts, and quickly found employment. An article in the June 5, 1865, edition of the *Springfield Republican* announced that Levy and a partner named Mayer had purchased Beran & Horner Dry Goods and added that "L. Karpeles, formerly of the old firm, is associated with a new one, and invites his old friends to see him there."

The disabled soldier took up residence in a boardinghouse at 299½ Main Street near the store's location at Main and State. Despite his warm welcome in the city, he did not remain in Springfield for long. While in Mount Pleasant General Hospital, Karpeles had met a former Union chaplain who was now the rabbi and shohet (ritual butcher) of Washington Hebrew Congregation. Rabbi Simon Mundheim, his wife Hannah, and their two daughters, Sarah and Henrietta, had often visited the hospital to read to the patients, write letters for them, and provide other care.

During one of the visits from the Mundheims, Karpeles learned that, even though doctors were preparing to amputate his leg, they thought there was a possibility that the leg might be saved with full-time home care. Karpeles went home with the Mundheims, the leg was saved, and Sarah and Leopold fell in love. They wanted to marry immediately, but Rabbi Mundheim asked them to wait for one year because of Sarah's young age of sixteen. Karpeles did not wait the full year and, with the rabbi's permission and performing of the ceremony, married Sarah before the end of 1865.

The couple had two children over the next five years, but Sarah and their third child died in childbirth on February 12, 1870. Henrietta moved into the Karpeles home at 1102 5th Street to care for the surviving children, and they too fell in love; on March 22, 1871, the two married, again with Rabbi Mundheim officiating. The couple had six additional children, three sons and three daughters.

While Karpeles settled into living in Washington, DC, he began efforts to finally receive the Medal of Honor for his valor in the Wilderness battle. In his 1870 affidavit applying for the medal, Karpeles wrote,

Your Applicant . . . states that while, his Regiment was engaged in the Battle of the Wilderness on the 6th day of May, 1864, at 5 o'clock P.M., Col., Bartlett commanding said regiment having been wounded, Lieutenant Colonel Charles S. Chandler of said Regiment assumed command. When after 5 o'clock on the 6th day of May, 1864, the right of the 9th Corps commenced breaking and falling back in considerable disorder, the rebels having commenced a flanking movement . . . your applicant being Regimental Color Bearer . . . inquired of the Lieutenant Colonel what was the matter. When he the Lieutenant Colonel, answered that he did not know what was the cause of the disorderly retreat of a portion of the Wing aforesaid. When your applicant urged him to stand firm and rally as many of the retreating troops as possible, he said, "All right, I will stand by you." We then, by every possible exertion, by waving the colors and otherwise, were enabled to rally a large number of retreating troops around our Regimental Colors.... When they were formed into a line and ordered to advance on the advancing Rebels, they, by a rapid discharge of fire arms, managed to check the enemy and enabled the disordered Wing to form, thereby, as your Applicant believes, saved that portion of the Wing aforesaid from almost total destruction, in which engagement our Colors were very severely shattered.

Letters from eyewitnesses, including his officers and fellow soldiers, accompanied the application. On April 30, 1870, a little more than two months after Sarah's death, Karpeles finally received his Medal of Honor.

Despite the lingering effects from his wounds, Karpeles, with support from his former officers and Massachusetts elected officials, secured a job with the Treasury Department and later the Postal Department. He remained active in Grand Army of the Republic reunions as well as gatherings of Jewish veterans of the conflict. His home was always open to fellow veterans visiting the capitol city. On April 23, 1890, Karpeles joined six other recipients to form the Medal of Honor Legion, a predecessor of today's Medal of Honor Foundation. The legion's letterhead stated eligibility to the group as being "Personal Identity, Legal Possession of the Medal, and Good Character."

In addition to promoting the legion and veterans activities, Karpeles also took an active role in defending his and other veterans' right to be treated fairly regardless of their disability. On December 19, 1899, Karpeles brought a lawsuit against the Metropolitan Railroad Company for injuries alleged to have occurred while exiting one of its cars.

By the time he filed his lawsuit, Karpeles was already in failing health. Unfortunately, his physical ailments from his leg wounds now affected his mental health. For more than a decade he was successful in getting the amount of his invalid pension increased. Claim documents of November 2, 1891, and March 24, 1892, both focus on his emotional state. The latter document stated that he suffered "increased disability of partial paralysis caused by gunshot wound. The paralysis now affects the brain, at times incapacitating him from work, and causing him loss of pay."

Karpeles made friends with many politicians and government workers in Washington, including Pres. William McKinley. His daughter Tasy later said,

"Father knew absolutely everyone from the President on down as far back as I can remember." He also conversed with foreign ambassadors and visiting officials from other countries in one of the five languages he spoke fluently—English, German, French, Greek, and Czech.

When the Spanish-American War broke out in 1898, Karpeles, according to family members, approached the president and volunteered to enlist to fight in Cuba despite the lingering effects from his Civil War wounds and his advancing age. He said to the president, "If I can no longer march—I can still ride a horse." President McKinley turned down the offer, saying, "You did your part, this is work for younger men."

Karpeles died on February 22, 1909, at the age of seventy in Washington's Garfield Hospital of complications from surgery to remove a malignant obstruction of the bowel. His death certificate states that at the time of his death he lived at 1102 5th Street NW in Washington. He is buried in the Washington Hebrew Congregation Cemetery. Henrietta died on July 12, 1925, and is buried at his side. His son Simon (1880–1950) served as a medical doctor in World War I and is buried in Arlington National Cemetery in Washington, DC. His grandson, Leopold M. (1921–2016), also became a doctor after serving as an enlisted sailor during World War II.

The bullet-pierced colors that Karpeles carried at the Wilderness are on display in the Massachusetts Hall of Flags. His medal, ammunition belt, saddlebag, documents, and photographs were put on special exhibit in 1959 at the B'nai B'rith Museum in Washington, DC. Karpeles's original medal was destroyed by fire. Its replacement is now at the Connecticut Valley Historical Museum in Springfield, Massachusetts. The B'nai B'rith Texas State Association issued a US Postal First Day Cover honoring Karpeles at its convention during the International Exposition known as Hemisphere '68 on March 30 in San Antonio. On May 5, 1989, Springfield's Connecticut Valley Historical Museum and Freedman Post 26 of the Jewish War Veterans of the United States of America honored Karpeles with a ceremony and program.

Throughout his life, Karpeles maintained contact with old friends from the 57th Massachusetts Infantry. A letter from one of his former officers perhaps best summarizes the importance of their service during the war and its aftermath. On June 1, 1888, 1st Lt. John Anderson of the 18th Infantry at Fort Gibson, Indian Territory (Oklahoma), wrote to Karpeles, "I was very glad to hear from you and glad to find you still on the shores of mortality where our numbers are fast diminishing. Our duty now lies in planting the principles and memory of the great struggle in the hearts of generations to follow us, endear the flag to them that you carried so faithfully and gallantly from the Wilderness to North Anna, and teach them to love the country which was saved at such a sacrifice."

★★★

4

David Arrin Urbansky,
Civil War, US Army

Company B, 58th Ohio Volunteer Infantry Regiment

Shiloh, Tennessee, April 7, 1862, and Vicksburg, Mississippi,
  December 28, 1862

Date Presented: August 2, 1879

CITATION:
Gallantry in actions.

DAVID URBANSKY earned his Medal of Honor in two of the Civil War's largest operations. Both his parents were born in Prussia; Louis in 1820 and Bertha Horwitz in 1822. David was born sometime in 1843 in Lautenburg, Prussia, and immigrated to the United States with his parents and five siblings in 1857. The family settled in New York State, where the senior Urbansky worked as a cabinetmaker for several years, before moving to Columbus, Ohio, where he established a mercantile business.

Urbansky worked alongside his father before enlisting in Company B, 58th Ohio Volunteer Infantry Regiment at Camp Chase in Columbus on October 21, 1861, for a three-year commitment. He was not the only Jew in the regiment, as Ohio provided more Jewish soldiers to the Civil War than any other state except New York. Various documents in his military files—some of which incorrectly list the spelling of his name as Orbansky—state that he stood five feet three inches tall, with a dark complexion, black hair, and brown eyes. One of his fellow enlistees described him as "a stout, hearty young man."

The 58th saw its initial action in the successful attack against Fort Donelson, Tennessee, on February 14–16, 1862. It then fought at the Battle of Shiloh on March 6–7 as a part of the 3rd Division, commanded by Gen. Lew Wallace under the Army of the Tennessee, led by Gen. Ulysses S. Grant. The 3rd Division did not reach the battlefield until the fighting had ceased on its first day. The next morning it participated in the counterattack that retook the original Union positions. No records have survived that detail Urbansky's heroism at Shiloh other than he performed with "gallantry in action."

From Shiloh, the 58th Ohio participated in the siege of Corinth, Mississippi, on April 29–May 30. During the remainder of 1862, the 58th and Urbansky conducted operations in Arkansas and Louisiana. In late December 1862, the 58th joined Gen. William T. Sherman's army in its offensive against the southern stronghold of Vicksburg that controlled traffic on the Mississippi River. By May 18, the Union army had Vicksburg surrounded and lay siege to the city. Vicksburg held out until July 4, but not until several battles had taken place in the surrounding area.

It was in one of the earliest fights for control of Vicksburg that Urbansky added to his record of valor that began at Shiloh. On December 27–29, the Union army attempted a direct assault at Chickasaw Bayou to capture the river city. The Confederates turned back each advance, including the major attack on the last day of the battle. In the midst of the shot and shell, Urbansky's company commander fell wounded as his unit retreated. When Urbansky saw that the captain lay unable to move, he returned to the main battlefield and, despite heavy rifle and cannon fire, carried the wounded officer to safety.

That evening, General Sherman stated he was "generally satisfied with the high spirit manifested" by his men despite their failure to push back the Confederates. His subordinate commanders also praised the performance of their men. Gen. James B. McPherson, commander of the XVII Corps, specifically noted the bravery of Urbansky and awarded him some form of medal. A notation dated July 1, 1879, in the records of the Adjutant General's Office of the War Department states that Urbansky had been awarded a "Medal of Silver" inscribed "Fort Donelson, Shiloh, Arkansas Post, Chickasaw Bayou, Grand Gulf, Fort Gibson, Vicksburg." It was presented on April 4, 1864, "under the terms and general order No.30, Headquarters, 17th Army Corps dated October 2, 1863."

It is likely that this Medal of Silver was an award originated by General McPherson and unique to his corps. In 1879, with the assistance of his congressman, Urbansky requested a replacement medal because the Medal of Silver had been lost. S. N. Benjamin, assistant adjutant general of the War Department, responded on August 1, writing, "Sir—replying to the application in your behalf from Hon. B. F. LeFevre, Member of Congress, I respectfully inform you that a duplicate of the medal awarded you by a Board of Honor under the direction of the late Major General McPherson, Commander 17th Army Corps, cannot be furnished by this office. The Secretary of War, however, directed that you be granted a Medal of Honor under the Act of Congress of July 12, 1862 which is herewith respectfully transmitted."

Urbansky's citation notes only the brief "gallantry in actions." The plural "actions" and the locations of Shiloh and Vicksburg show that the medal was for the dual valorous actions. Acts of bravery and the rewards for merit, however, did not end, or even ease, the trials and tribulations of the Civil War infantryman—even if not directly involved in battle. The 58th Ohio and Urbansky saw little combat after the victory at Vicksburg as they performed "Provost duty" or occupation responsibilities until the end of their enlistment. During this time, according to later documents supporting his claim for a disability pension, Urbansky contracted rheumatism and heart disease, which eventually led to kidney and liver problems due to exposure in the field and in camp.

Urbansky and the other surviving original volunteers of the 58th Ohio returned to Columbus in late 1864, where they were formally mustered out at Camp Chase on January 14, 1865. During its three-year-plus service, the regiment lost 305 officers and men to combat, accidents, and disease.

Apparently, Urbansky did not perform all his duties as well as he displayed bravery on the battlefield. He left the army at the same rank he entered—private. Regimental records of the 58th Ohio note that he was promoted to corporal on January 8, 1862, only a little more than two months after his enlistment. Three months later, on April 8, he was reduced in rank back to private, a rank he held for the remainder of his time in uniform. No reason for this reduction is included in his records.

Shortly after his discharge, Urbansky applied for and received his US citizenship. He had fought the entire war as a noncitizen immigrant. Urbansky then traveled to Schenectady, New York, where he married Rachel Henry in a

Jewish wedding on October 8, 1865, with Rabbi Isaac Gotthard officiating. His ketubah (a Jewish prenuptial agreement or contract) translates his Hebrew name as Aaron David Urbansky.

The newly married couple resided in Toledo, Ohio, for nearly three years before moving to Piqua in western Ohio in 1869, where they established a successful clothing store. They prospered financially as their family grew with the arrival of twelve children. Urbansky was known to be modest about his personal bravery in the war, but he was active in organizations that supported and celebrated the service of his fellow veterans. He was a charter member of Piqua's Grand Army of the Republic Alexander Post 158, established on November 9, 1881.

The former soldier had continued suffering the lingering effects from his war service on his heart and liver. Urbansky began a serious decline in 1894, remaining in poor health until his death on January 22, 1897, at age fifty-four at his home at 231 W. Water Street in Piqua. His funeral was held at his family home, conducted by Reform rabbi David Phillipson, the spiritual leader of K. K. Bene Israel (now Rockdale Temple) in Cincinnati. Fellow members of his GAR post attended en masse. Also present were his fellow Masons of Warren Lodge 24, Free and Accepted Masons. The lodge published a resolution that read, "[W]e shall cherish his memory with kindest recollection and imitate his virtues in the highest appreciation of their merits."

Urbansky was buried in Piqua's Cedar Hill Cemetery. After his death, Rachel and the children moved to Cincinnati. She resided at 431 Forest Avenue until her death on January 15, 1925. After her interment in Walnut Hills Cemetery, the family had David's remains moved from Piqua and placed beside her. A daughter, Miriam Urban, who was retired from the faculty of the University of Cincinnati and died in 1977, is buried next to her mother.

Rachel was buried and David reburied under the name Urban, a form that the family had adopted. This, along with the two original spellings, Urbansky and Orbansky, caused difficulties for researchers trying to locate gravesites of Medal of Honor recipients. The graves were finally located in 2000, and on December 10, a Medal of Honor Veterans Affairs headstone was added to the grave. A Civil War reenactment group served as an honor guard. Rabbi Mark N. Goldman, senior rabbi at Rockdale Temple and a successor to Rabbi Phillipson, who conducted Urbansky's original funeral, led the Jewish prayers at the headstone's dedication. The Pique Public Library added Urbansky to its Hall of Fame in 2009.

Urbansky's Medal of Honor is in the Jacob Rader Marcus Center of the American Jewish Archives in Cincinnati.

★★★

5

Simon Suhler (Charles Gardner),
Indian Wars, US Army

Company B, 8th U. S. Cavalry Regiment

Arizona, August–October 1868

Date Presented: July 24, 1869

CITATION:
Bravery in scout and actions against Indians.

SIMON SUHLER fought in two wars under three different names, suffered at least three wounds, survived as a prisoner of war, withstood being accused of desertion, and earned his adopted country's highest decoration for valor. Little is known of his early life other than he was born to impoverished parents sometime in 1844 in Marksteft, Bavaria. He and his three siblings were orphaned in 1858, and Simon managed to immigrate to the United States while still in his early teens.

The first remaining record of Suhler's arrival in the United States is when he enlisted in the 32nd Indiana Volunteer Infantry Regiment at Lafayette on August 24, 1861, at age seventeen. Composed mostly of German immigrants and descendants of local German settlers, the regiment was known as the "First German." A graduate of the Potsdam Military School, its commander, Col. August Willich, was a thirteen-year veteran in the Prussian army as an artillery officer. On December 17, the 32nd saw its first combat at Rowlett's Station, Kentucky, and earned recognition for its stand against a Confederate attack and the killing of Col. Benjamin F. Terry, commander of Terry's Texas Rangers.

On April 6, the 32nd Indiana joined the fight at Shiloh, Tennessee, where Suhler was slightly wounded during the first day of fighting. The next day he suffered a serious wound when a musket ball passed through his left leg just below the knee. He was evacuated to a hospital in St. Louis, Missouri, then to Evansville, Indiana, and finally to Simons General Hospital in Mound City, Illinois.

Suhler recovered sufficiently to rejoin his regiment for the Battle of Chicka-mauga, where he was captured by the Confederates near Jasper, Tennessee, on August 22, 1862. He was held at Vicksburg until he was paroled on September 1, 1862, and transferred to a Union parole installation at Camp Chase, Ohio. Such camps had been established by the two belligerents early in the war when both sides took many more prisoners than they had facilities to house and care for. Parole agreements stated that prisoners released would not again take up arms against those who captured them for a set time or until they were exchanged for prisoners of the other sides. Confederate prisoners frequently awaited exchange in their homes while Union parolees were often kept in facilities, such as Camp Chase, in somewhat austere conditions, until their formal exchange.

Apparently, Suhler did not like the confinement to camp, or perhaps he just yearned to return to the fight. Regardless of his motives, the muster roll of the 32nd Indiana for the period of January–February 1863 states that Suhler had been a prisoner of war waiting for exchange at Camp Chase since August 1862. The subsequent muster roll for March–April 1863 shows Suhler as "Deserted March 17, 1863, from Parole Camp Carrington" near Indianapolis, Indiana. Muster rolls for the 32nd Indiana continued to list Suhler as a deserter until the unit was mustered out after the end of the war.

Fewer than three months after deserting, Suhler volunteered for a three-year enlistment in Company A, 11th New York Heavy Artillery Regiment at Buffalo, New York, under the name of Simon Newstattel—his mother's maiden name—on June 9, 1863. His enlistment papers indicate that he was eighteen years and six months of age; stood five feet six and a half inches tall; had gray eyes, brown hair, and a fair complextion; and was left-handed; his civilian occupation was "tailor." Thomas McDonough of Buffalo signed the enlistment papers as Simon's "guardian." As this is the only record of any re-lationship between McDonough and Suhler/Newstattel, it would not be out of line to speculate that the document, like his new name, was not entirely honest or aboveboard.

Artillery was classified by the Union army during the Civil War as heavy or light, depending on the maneuverability and size of the guns. Teams of horses moved light or field artillery pieces in both offensive and defensive operations. Heavy artillery, on the other hand, was used primarily in defending fixed fortifications or for siege operations. Union heavy artillery saw little action as it mostly occupied fortifications defending Washington, DC.

Companies of the 11th New York, including Newstattel's, transferred to the 4th New York Heavy Artillery Regiment on July 25, 1863. Newstattel, assigned as a private in Company I, joined the defense of the nation's capital. In the spring of 1864, Gen. Ulysses S. Grant determined that there was no longer a significant threat to Washington and reassigned various heavy artillery units, including the 4th New York, to duties as infantrymen.

The 4th New York fought as infantrymen in the battles of the Wilderness, Spotsylvania, North Anna, and Cold Harbor, as well as the siege of Petersburg and the Appomattox Campaign. No records of Newstattel's service, other than being listed as "Present" on the regiment's muster rolls, remain. Following the surrender of Gen. Robert E. Lee at Appomattox, the 4th New York marched to Washington, DC, where they participated in the Grand Review of the Armies on May 23. The 4th New York Heavy Artillery lost a total of 454 men during the Civil War: 8 officers and 108 enlisted men were killed or mortally wounded (most while fighting as infantrymen), 4 officers and 343 enlisted men died of disease.

The regiment then remained in camp around the capital city until it and Newstattel were mustered out of the army on September 26, 1865. The last record of Newstattel prior to his honorable discharge reports that he was "on duty at Angus General Hospital since August 13, 1865" in Washington, DC. Since he is listed as on duty rather than as a patient, it can be assumed that he was an orderly or served some other support role at the hospital.

Suhler/Newstattel was not one to remain in one place for long. Like many Civil War veterans, he headed west soon after his discharge. By the time he reached San Francisco in the fall of 1866, he had spent his mustering-out pay of nearly $80. He was out of funds and out of work. Suhler therefore turned to a profession he knew best. On October 15, he enlisted in B Troop, 8th United States Cavalry as a private under the name Charles Gardner at the Presidio of San Francisco. Despite the distance to the army records centers back east, Suhler likely changed his name for the third time to avoid any connection to his still-pending charge of desertion. As for the name itself, there was a Charles Gardner in the 4th New York Heavy Artillery at the same time Suhler/Newstattel served in the regiment.

The twelve troops of the 8th Cavalry were widely scattered, being stationed at forts and camps in California, Oregon, Washington, Idaho, and Nevada to protect settlements and roadways from Native American uprisings. Gardner's B Troop initially served at Camp Cadiz, California, before transferring in 1867 to Arizona Territory with three other companies to combat Apaches, Hualapais, and Navajos. There is no record of Gardner's specific performance during this period other than he was present and served honorably. This in itself is commendable because of the high desertion rate in the regiment at the time.

Skirmishes with the Indians intensified in the summer and fall of 1868 in Arizona Territory with B Troop almost constantly in the saddle on patrol. On August 22, B Troop killed two Indians and captured another along the Santa Maria River and on September 9 killed two Hualapais and captured four more. The next day the cavalrymen killed an additional four and captured three others as well as a large amount of provisions and camp equipment. On the 11th, the troop killed five more hostiles and captured more supplies.

B Troop surprised a band of Tonto Apaches near the mouth of the Dragoon Fork of the Verde River on the 13th and killed two and captured weapons and food. Gardner suffered a wound in the fight. A Department of Arizona document dated October 31, 1868, stated that 2nd Lt. Rufus Somerby led a scouting operation composed of thirty-one troopers from B and L Troops and three civilian guides on August 13 to October 31. In the report Somerby summarized the operation and singled out Gardner, stating that he "deserves special favor for fighting after receiving an almost fatal wound" at Rio Verde, Arizona, when an arrow struck him in the left side of his chest.

On December 7, 1868, Bvt. Maj. Gen. Edward O. C. Ord, commander of the Department of the Pacific, sent a letter to Somerby breveting him to the rank of 1st lieutenant and commending the officer and his cavalrymen "for their energy and efficiency." General Ord also recommended that Gardner be "presented with a medal for special bravery in the field" and requested that the cavalryman's commander forward the necessary paperwork to the secretary of war for his promotion to 2nd lieutenant.

The promotion of Gardner never occurred for unknown reasons, but it is likely that he turned down the promotion in fear that his former record and his enlistment under an alias might be revealed. Actions for the awarding of a medal, however, continued. In early 1869 a series of letters between Ord and

Bvt. Maj. Gen. Edward D. Townsend, adjutant general of the US Army, debated whether to award Gardner the Medal of Honor and the other members of the patrol a Certificate of Merit.

General Townsend wrote to Ord on April 29, 1869, "There are plenty of Medals (of Honor) stored in the War Department which might be conferred on these men if deemed proper." Ord deemed that they were proper, and on June 3 Townsend reported that Gen. William T. Sherman, commander in chief of the US Army, and John A. Rawlins, secretary of war, had approved Medals of Honor for all members of the patrol. The medals were sent with a transmittal letter to Ord on July 7 and awarded to Gardner and the other cavalrymen on July 24. This relatively brief time from recommendation to award resulted in Gardner's receiving his Medal of Honor before several of his fellow Jewish Americans received theirs for their Civil War heroism.

Gardner completed his three-year enlistment and was honorably discharged as a private at Fort Stanton, New Mexico, on October 15, 1871. Two years later, either out of a continued sense of adventure or from the difficulties of unemployment, Suhler/Newstattel/Gardner enlisted as a private, again under the name Gardner, in Troop M, 6th Cavalry Regiment, on September 6, 1873. The 6th Cavalry operated primarily out of Fort Sill, Indian Territory (Oklahoma), against Cheyennes, Kiowas, and Comanches. In April 1874, Gardner transferred back to his old outfit of B Troop, 8th Cavalry. The 8th Calvary opposed the same Indian tribes as the 6th Cavalry before moving to Texas to conduct security operations along the Rio Grande. Gardner advanced in rank to sergeant before once again accepting an honorable discharge on September 12, 1877.

The next record of Suhler is in 1883 in San Antonio, Texas, where, according to city documents, he resumed his birth name and worked as a produce dealer and later sold sewing machines and lightning rods. From 1892 to 1893, he was the Bexar County tax assessor and then worked as a bookkeeper until 1895.

During his years in San Antonio, Suhler was a member of the A. Belknap Post 37 of the GAR. He also began efforts to have his desertion charge from the parole camp dismissed and to receive a pension for his service as Suhler as well as Newstattel. Suhler gained success in the former, but not the latter. On January 25, 1890, the War Department issued a letter signed by the assistant surgeon of the US Army stating, "By direction of the Secretary of War, I have the honor to inform you that the charge of desertion of March 17, 1863, standing against Simon Suhler, as of Company G, 32nd Indiana Volunteers, has been removed from his record in this Department. He is discharged to date March 17, 1863."

Simon's older brother, Aron, who had immigrated to the United States in 1871 and reconnected with Simon in San Antonio, assisted in the efforts. Aron, an ordained rabbi, initially settled in Akron, Ohio, before moving to Dallas in 1875, where he became the first Reform rabbi in the state of Texas. He moved briefly to Vicksburg, Mississippi, before returning to Texas in 1884 and taking up residence in Waco, from where he submitted an affidavit on November 28, 1891, supporting his brother's claims for a pension for service in the Civil War as both Simon Suhler and Simon Newstattel. Simon also retained James S. Duffie, a Washington, DC, attorney to support his claim. Requests to the Auditor's Office of the Department of the Treasury produced a letter saying that it could not conclusively confirm by a study of signatures and other documents that Suhler and Newstattel were the same soldier.

Suhler, from his home at 325 South Harris Street in San Antonio, continued his efforts to receive his pension based on his service under his real name and Newstattel and Gardner. He made a claim with the Bureau of Pensions that was filed on August 26, 1893. Before final action was taken, he died at his home of heart disease on May 16, 1895, at age fifty-one. He is buried in San Antonio National Cemetery (Section I, Grave 1610). He never married and left behind no children. Although there is a painting of what Suhler might have looked like, there is no existing photograph or other accurate image of Suhler.

The veteran of the infantry, artillery, and cavalry lay mostly unrecognized and unremembered for nearly a century before Medal of Honor researchers and descendants of Aron Suhler finally uncovered the entire story of Suhler/Newstattel/Gardner. On November 11, 1987, the 5th US Army band played taps, and an honor guard presented a twenty-one-gun salute at the formal dedication of the Medal of Honor headstone honoring Suhler. William Suhler, grandson of Aron, unveiled the marker. In attendance were representatives of fifteen veterans groups and forty-three relatives of Simon from all over the world, including three Holocaust survivors from France.

6

Samuel Gross (Samuel Margulies),
Haitian Campaign, US Marine Corps

23rd Company, US Marine Corps, USS Connecticut

Fort Rivière, Haiti, November 17, 1915

Date Presented: September 17, 1917

CITATION:

In company with members of the 5th, 13th, 23d Companies and the marine and sailor detachment from the U.S.S. Connecticut, Gross participated in the attack on Fort Riviere, Haiti, 17 November 1915. Following a concentrated drive, several different detachments of marines gradually closed in on the old French bastion fort in an effort to cut off all avenues of retreat for the Caco bandits. Approaching a breach in the wall, which was the only entrance to the fort, Gross was the second man to pass through the breach in the face of constant fire from the Cacos and, thereafter, for a 10-minute period, engaged the enemy in desperate hand-to-hand combat until the bastion was captured and Caco resistance neutralized.

SAMUEL MARGULIES falsified his age and changed his name to volunteer for the US Marine Corps. He later fought alongside one of the most famous marines in history to earn his Medal of Honor. Margulies ran away from his authoritarian father's home in his birthplace of Philadelphia in early 1913 and fled to New York State. In Buffalo he met a marine recruiter who directed him to Norfolk, Virginia, where Margulies enlisted in the Marine Corps as a private on June 2, 1913, under the name of Samuel Gross with a birth date of May 9, 1891. Family members later estimated that his birth year was more likely 1897, making Samuel only sixteen years of age when he enlisted. Samuel's family members have no explanation for the selection of his alias, and the marine himself never explained why he selected the name Gross, under which he lived for the remainder of his life.

Private Gross participated in the US occupation of Veracruz during the Mexican Revolution from April 23 to December 5, 1914. He arrived in the port city only a day after Maj. Smedley D. Butler earned his first Medal of Honor by leading a battalion of marines to secure the town. Sometime during the following weeks, Butler selected Gross as his personal orderly. When Butler returned to his regular duty station and home in Panama, Gross accompanied him as his personal orderly and became devoted to the major as well as his wife and children.

On July 28, 1915, Haitian president Vilbrun Guillaume Sam, the fifth leader of the country in only five years, was deposed and killed by a mob of bandit-guerillas called Cacos. US president Woodrow Wilson, attempting to spread democracy in the Caribbean and following his policy of not recognizing non-democratic governments while also fearing possible interference by Germany in the island's politics, dispatched naval ships with marines aboard to stabilize the country. Wilson said, "We consider it our duty to insist on constitutional government there, and will, if necessary, if they force us to it as the only way, take charge of elections and see that a real government is elected which we can support."

Smedley Butler commanded the marines with Samuel Gross at his side as his orderly. On August 10, Butler, Gross, and about 100 marines and sailors from the USS *Connecticut* went ashore on Haiti. In October, Butler began offensive operations from his base at Le Trou that pushed the Cacos—formidable fighters and brutal in their treatment of dead and captured marines and sailors—farther back into the mountains. One of Butler's lieutenants was killed and beheaded by the rebels, leading Butler to declare later that Haiti was "a bloody crazy Garden of Eden."

By mid-November the marines and sailors had captured all of the Caco fortifications with the exception of Fort Rivière, an old French-built stronghold at the top of Montagne Noire. The Americans surrounded the fort, looking for an entrance through its rock-wall defenses. Sgt. Ross L. Iams found a breach in the wall and plunged through to the fort's interior. Butler tried to go next, but Gross stepped in and preceded his boss into the fight. The battle lasted only about ten minutes, with the marines killing, in what became hand-to-hand combat, between ten and fifty-one Cacos, the number varying in the many later accounts.

After the fight, Butler commended Iams and Gross and recommended them for medals. Gross remained in Haiti for another year, keeping the peace and combating remaining rebels in the jungle and mountains. On December 2, 1916, he was promoted to corporal and on February 5, 1917, was transferred to Marine Barracks, Philadelphia. Although he was back in his hometown, there is no evidence that Gross attempted to contact his family. On May 24 he received an honorable discharge from the Marine Corps.

The commandant of the Marine Corps, Maj. Gen. George Barnett, sent a letter to Gross from his headquarters in Washington, DC, on September 17, 1917. Barnett wrote, "It affords me great pleasure to forward you, by registered mail, a Medal of Honor awarded you for your conspicuous coolness and bravery in entering Fort Riviere, Haiti, on November 17, 1915, while serving with the 23rd Company of Marines, when such action on your part seemed almost certain would result in your being instantly killed or at least dangerously wounded. I trust that you will wear the medal with much gratification and pride during the years to come."

Iams and Butler also received Medals of Honor for the fight. Butler is one of only nineteen men to receive the medal twice—all awarded prior to World War II.

Gross reenlisted in the Marine Corps on March 8, 1918, at the height of US involvement in World War I. The hero of Haiti did not, however, participate in the conflict. On September 10, 1918, the Marine Corps medically discharged Gross at Marine Barracks, Washington, DC, because of epilepsy that resulted from wounds he suffered in Haiti. He remained hospitalized for the rest of his life. Marcus Margulies, Gross's brother, found him after several years of search in Washington's St. Elizabeth Hospital. He moved Samuel to the veterans hospital in Coatesville, Pennsylvania, so the veteran would be closer to his remaining family.

Butler, who lost track of his former orderly, retired in Newtown Square just west of Philadelphia in 1931. There he entered politics and traveled the country giving lectures. In 1933 he spoke at the Coatesville Veterans Hospital and included the story of the attack on Fort Rivière, mentioning in particular the courage of Gross. At the conclusion of his remarks, a nurse wheeled an emaciated figure up to the general. Gathering his strength, Gross said,

"Corporal Gross reporting, sir." Butler immediately recognized his old orderly and, with tears in his eyes, returned the salute. Following the emotional reunion, the two talked for hours, remembering their time together in the Corps and in combat.

The old general made frequent visits to his former orderly in the hospital before Gross died on September 13, 1934. Gross was buried in Philadelphia's Har-Nebo Jewish Cemetery with only a few family members, Butler, and the general's oldest son attending.

According to cemetery records, the Margulies family paid an annual fee of $6 for the upkeep of Gross's grave for only three years before family members either died or ran out of money in the midst of the Depression. Cemetery officials efficiently noted the grave's location in their records, but Samuel Margulies/Gross lay in an unmarked grave for nearly a half century before Medal of Honor researchers rediscovered it in 1983 and made arrangements for him to receive a VA headstone. The researchers also found that Gross did not make a big thing out of being a Medal of Honor recipient; rather, he was "a quiet hero." More importantly, he was remembered as "a good Marine."

On May 29, 1983, members of Philadelphia's Drizin Weiss Post 215 of the Jewish War Veterans of the United States of America dedicated the headstone. The ceremony included the placing of the flag, the laying of a wreath, a reading of the Kaddish, the firing of a Marine Color Guard salute, and the playing of taps. There is no known surviving photograph of Gross. A stylized painting by Maj. Donna Neary of the storming of Fort Rivière by Gross, Iams, and Butler is held by the Marine Corps History Division.

★★★

7

Sydney Gustave Gumpertz,
World War I, US Army

Company E, 132nd Infantry Regiment, 33rd Infantry Division

Bois de Forges, France, September 9, 1918

Date Presented: February 9, 1919

CITATION:

When the advancing line was held up by machinegun fire, 1st Sgt. Gumpertz left the platoon of which he was in command and started with two other soldiers through a heavy barrage toward the machinegun nest. His two companions soon became casualties from bursting shells, but 1st Sgt. Gumpertz continued on alone in the face of direct fire from the machinegun, jumped into the nest and silenced the gun, capturing 9 of the crew.

SYDNEY GUMPERTZ was nearly forty years of age, with no prior military experience, when he volunteered to fight as an infantryman in World War I. Within fifteen months, he advanced in rank to 1st sergeant of his company and earned his country's highest award for valor.

Born on October 24, 1879, in San Rafael, California, Gumpertz came from a family of merchants and soldiers. His grandfather immigrated to the United States from Europe and crossed the country to the Pacific Coast in 1850 to sell provisions, clothes, and equipment to the mining camps from a mule-drawn wagon. His father established a general store in Stockton, California, that continued to provide merchandise to the miners of the Mother Lode. On his mother's side, Gumpertz's great-grandfather, a Jew from Alsace, had fought all over Europe as a member of Napoleon Bonaparte's guard.

Gumpertz grew up in Stockton and drilled as a member of his high school cadet corps before his family moved to New York City, where he completed his education. After graduating from high school, he became a newspaperman, alternating between reporting and management. Not one to remain in one place for long, Gumpertz moved on to Oregon and Washington before returning to his native California. He finally settled in 1913 in Chicago, where he met Anna Light, a traveling vaudeville stage actress.

Much of what we know of Gumpertz's life comes from an interview conducted by James Hopper, author of *Medals of Honor*, which appeared in a chapter titled "Through Hell to Glory." Published in 1929, the article says that Gumpertz recalled that he followed Anna from town to town. He said, "I proposed to her in at least twenty-four towns and cities. I chased her all over the United States for two years. And then, I guess she said yes simply because I had worn her out."

Sydney and Anna married in 1915 and settled in Chicago at 57 E. Van Buren Street. The couple attended a rally on Michigan Avenue in July 1917 where uniformed men spoke to the crowd about the US involvement in war in Europe. Despite being thirty-eight years old, Sydney talked the situation over with Anna and the next day went to the local armory of the 2nd Illinois Infantry Regiment, a unit under the broad umbrella of the newly designated National Guard that had replaced militia units the previous year.

In the Hopper interview eleven years after his enlistment, the author asked why he was so anxious to enlist. Gumpertz replied, "Well, because I'm a patriot. I don't know why, but I've always been. I, well, I'm willing to give my life to my country."

Hopper then asked Anna about her thoughts on Sydney's volunteering. She answered, "I wouldn't have much use for any man who wouldn't fight for his country."

When Gumpertz reported for enlistment, he failed the physical because of a hernia. Undeterred, he checked into a hospital the next morning and had a successful operation. That afternoon, he was sworn into active duty.

Gumpertz and the 2nd Illinois, activated on July 21, boarded a train to Camp Logan in Houston, Texas, for training. There they were reorganized as the 132nd Infantry Regiment on October 12 as a part of the 33rd Infantry Division (the Prairie Division). Because of his military bearing at six feet tall, his maturity, and his leadership abilities, Gumpertz was appointed 1st sergeant of Company E of the 132nd.

Anna joined Sydney in Houston but returned to Chicago when the 33rd Division boarded trains on May 5, 1918, for the East Coast for embarkation to France. Gumpertz and his unit initially teamed with British units at Albert in the Somme and then joined Australians in the Battle of Hamel on July 4. Much of the fighting was hand-to-hand in the trenches. Gumpertz later described the performance of his men: "We had some tough bayonets in our company."

In August, the 33rd Division joined other American units on the St. Mihiel front and then took part in the offensive toward Metz on September 12–15. This was the first offensive of the war launched solely by American units and the first operation in which the terms "D-Day" and "H-Hour" were used.

Shortly after the battle, notice came from division headquarters that all Jewish soldiers were to be granted leave to go to the town of Bar-le-Duc to attend Yom Kippur services. These orders were suddenly rescinded, and the division marched to Mort Homme to relieve a French force on September 23. After a sustained artillery barrage on the morning of September 26, the 33rd Division went "over the top" in the Meuse-Argonne Offensive—the largest by the Americans in the war.

Gumpertz, leading a platoon of about fifty men, advanced through the fog-laden countryside into Bois de Forges, a formerly peaceful French forest that was now a devastated moonscape of splintered trees, shell holes, and dead bodies from both sides. Multiple German machine guns, supported by infantry and artillery, stood in the Americans' path. Gumpertz and his platoon overran the first German trench line, taking fifty prisoners. When they once again began to advance, a machine gun raked their ranks and drove the doughboys to the ground. Gumpertz called for two volunteers, and then the three began to crawl toward the machine-gun position. As they neared the Germans, the Americans rose and charged forward with bayonets fixed. Within seconds they captured the gun and another fourteen prisoners.

The platoon continued the advance only to be engaged by another machine gun a few minutes later. Gumpertz, accompanied by the same two volunteers, again went forward. This time they faced not only machine-gun fire but artillery and hand grenades as well. Both of his companions became casualties, but Gumpertz continued his attack until he captured the gun, killed several of its crew, and captured nine more Germans.

Gumpertz had earned his Medal of Honor, but the fight and the war were not yet over. His regiment continued the offensive on October 8 and crossed the Meuse to occupy Bois de Consenvoye after a protracted battle. Gumpertz suffered a wound in the fight but was able to rejoin his company for the final push into Luxemburg before the Armistice on November 11.

After the guns stopped firing, the 33rd Division went into camp waiting embarkation back home. On February 9, 1919, Gumpertz and sixteen other soldiers were awarded Medals of Honor by the commander of the American Expeditionary Force, Gen. John J. Pershing, at Chaumont, France—the largest such ceremony in the war. In addition to his Medal of Honor from his own country, Gumpertz was recognized for his valor by the governments of France and Italy.

The 132nd Infantry Regiment arrived back home to be demobilized at Camp Grant, Illinois, on May 31, 1919. Before his discharge, Gumpertz received an officer's commission and a promotion to captain.

Gumpertz settled in New York City, where he worked in advertising and public relations, became the commander of S. Rankin Drew Post 340 of the American Legion, and edited *The Legion Annual*. He also dabbled in politics. An article in the August 12, 1920, edition of the *New York Tribune* began with a summary of his actions in France that earned him the Medal of Honor. It then said, "It could never be suspected that he had nerves. But he has." The article further detailed that Gumpertz was a candidate to be a delegate to the state meeting at Albany. As the hours went by after the polls closed with no announcement of the results, according to the article, Gumpertz became more and more anxious and said to a friend, "Whew! This running for office is an awful strain."

In 1921, Gumpertz was named commander of the Jewish Valor Legion, which had been formed to counter negative comments on the patriotism of American Jews circulated by automobile magnate Henry Ford. He continued his efforts to publicize and promote the military service of Jews in his self-published book of 1934 titled *The Jewish Legion of Valor: The Story of Jewish Heroes in the Wars of the Republic and General History of Military Exploits of the Jews through the Ages*. The book was the most complete of its time and remains the best reference on the subject. It more than meets his objective, stated in his introduction, which reads, "The object of this book is to present the story of the Jew as a warrior; to describe his fighting activities throughout history in general, and during the World War in particular."

Gumpertz did not elaborate on his own bravery in the war in his book. Rather, he reprinted the interview conducted by James Hopper six years earlier and printed in his book *Medals of Honor.*

Gumpertz died at age ninety-one on February 16, 1971, after a lengthy stay at the veterans hospital in New York City. He is buried in Long Island National Cemetery (Section DSS, Site 65) at Farmington, New York, under a headstone with the Cross of David. According to his *New York Times* obituary, he was survived by his daughter, Florence Miller, and a sister, Ruth Rosenblatt. His Medal of Honor is at the National Museum of American Jewish Military History in Washington, DC. The Jacob Rader Marcus Center of the American Jewish Archives in Cincinnati, Ohio, has photographs of Gumpertz in its files.

8

Benjamin Kaufman,
World War I, US Army

Company K, 308th Infantry Regiment, 77th Infantry Division
Argonne Forest, France, October 4, 1918
Date Presented: April 8, 1919

CITATION:
He took out a patrol for the purpose of attacking an enemy machinegun which had checked the advance of his company. Before reaching the gun he became separated from his patrol and a machinegun bullet shattered his right arm. Without hesitation he advanced on the gun alone, throwing grenades with his left hand and charging with an empty pistol, taking one prisoner and scattering the crew, bringing the gun and prisoner back to the first-aid station.

BENJAMIN KAUFMAN went absent without leave from his hospital bed to rejoin his unit at the front and earn the Medal of Honor. After returning from the war, he dedicated his life to ensuring and promoting equality and justice for all people, regardless of race, creed, or religion.

Born on a farm near Buffalo, New York, on March 10, 1894, as one of six brothers and three sisters to parents Peter and Anna, Kaufman spent his early years doing chores and exploring the surrounding fields and woods. At age nine he and his family moved to Brooklyn, New York, where his father operated a livery stable. Benjamin assisted in the renting of horses and carriages and performed odd jobs. He attended PS 149 and Erasmus High School in Brooklyn before graduating from Newtown High School on Long Island, where he excelled in football, baseball, and basketball. He earned the reputation of a "scrapper" who stood up for the weak and bullied.

After graduating from high school, Kaufman attended Syracuse University on a partial athletic scholarship before dropping out to play professional baseball in the minor leagues. When the United States entered World War I, he enlisted in the National Guard on September 10, 1917. During his training at Camp Upton, New York, his unit was federalized as the 308th Infantry Regiment of the 77th Infantry Division, known as the "Metropolitan or Statue of Liberty Division" because a large number of its members came from the five boroughs of New York City. On February 4, 1918, the 308th was the first regiment from the National Guard to receive its regular army colors, and the troops paraded through New York City in celebration.

Kaufman made an impression on his officers as well as his fellow soldiers. He became the regimental boxing champion and his tenacious yet unassuming demeanor moved him up the ranks to corporal in September 1917, to sergeant the following February, and to 1st sergeant of K Company in June. "I guess I never quite fit the picture of the tough, hard-drinking first sergeant," he later recalled. But his men highly respected him. In the ranks he was known as "the best Top Kick in the A.E.F." His superiors twice recommended that he receive a direct commission, but because that meant he would have to transfer to another company, he turned down each offer in order to remain with his men.

The 77th Infantry Division embarked for France on April 6, 1917, and arrived on the 19th. They initially joined the British command for further training before being committed to the front line near the town of Badonviller in the Baccarat Sector in early June—one of the first former National Guard units to go into battle. The 308th Regiment became a veteran unit over the next two months with more than a third of its ranks either killed or wounded.

In August the 308th was pulled off-line to receive and train replacements. Most of the new men came from farms and ranches in the western United States. Kaufman, who previously had led mostly foreign-born or first-generation soldiers from the New York area, developed an even more acute awareness and understanding of different ethnic and cultural backgrounds.

At the end of the month, the 308th rejoined the fight in the Allied Aisne-Marne Offensive. While assisting in the evacuation of several of his wounded soldiers, Kaufman was blinded by a German artillery gas attack. He refused evacuation until he was sure his wounded had been taken care of. Kaufman did not remain in the hospital for long. Despite still having blurry vision, he borrowed a uniform, walked out of the hospital, and returned to K Company, where he was threatened with court martial for being absent without leave from the medical facility. The threat was not carried out, as the 1st sergeant was needed and welcomed.

During the Meuse-Argonne Offensive, the 77th Division attacked strongly held German positions in the Argonne Forest. Nine companies of doughboys pushed ahead of the rest of the division and on October 2 were isolated and surrounded by the Germans. Maj. Charles Whittlesey took command of what became known as the "Lost Battalion" as it fought on with little ammunition and almost no water or food for the next six days. Of the about 554 men, roughly 197 were killed in action and approximately 150 went missing or were taken prisoner before the 194 remaining men were rescued.

While the designation of "Lost Battalion" made for good headlines and news stories, the unit was not so much lost as cut off. Other US units, including K Company, attempted to go to their support and rescue. During their advance on October 4, Kaufman and two privates became separated from the rest of their unit and took fire from a German machine gun. Both privates fell wounded, and Kaufman took a bullet that shattered his right arm. Holding his pistol, now out of ammunition, in his right hand, he charged forward throwing hand grenades with his left. The surviving machine-gun crew scattered; one surrendered. Kaufman returned to his lines with the captured machine gun carried by his prisoner.

When later asked by a news reporter what it was like to be a hero, Kaufman said, "It's more of an accident than anything else. You do things you wouldn't ordinarily do. You go off your nut in battle."

Kaufman remained hospitalized for the remainder of the war. When he sufficiently recovered, he rejoined his regiment as it continued to train in France. On April 8, 1919, Gen. John J. Pershing presented the Medal of Honor to Kaufman. Other countries, including France, Italy, and Montenegro, also decorated the hero.

The 308th Regiment sailed for New York on April 19 aboard the USS *America*; the unit was demobilized at Camp Upton on May 9. Kaufman settled in Trenton, New Jersey, where he went into business and became active in civic and veterans organizations. He later said, "After the war, I had a wholesale paper and bag business. There was always something going because of speaking engagements. It took so much time I had to give up my business."

Kaufman joined the Veterans of Foreign Wars and the American Legion. He was also a member of the Medal of Honor Society. In 1931 he organized the Jewish War Veterans Post 156 in Trenton and served as the national commander of the Jewish War Veterans from 1941 to 1943 and as that organization's national executive director from 1948 to 1957.

In addition to assisting his fellow veterans, Kaufman supported children's organizations and combined that with his continued interest in baseball. After Kaufman's death, a friend in Trenton remembered, "Back in 1928 when the American Legion Junior Baseball program was started here, I wonder how many of those kids knew that the guy playing first base during their practice sessions held the country's highest honor. I doubt that Ben told them. He would mingle with the kids, encourage them, and was their greatest rooter. He loved them and they loved him. Not because he was a hero but because he took such interest in them."

Kaufman also served as the state commander of the Disabled Veterans of the World War (now Disabled American Veterans). He was a member of Trenton Welfare Commission and the Mayor's Citizen Committee. He was also active on the Crippled Children's Committee of the Trenton Lodge of Fraternal Order of Elks.

His primary occupation as director of the New Jersey Employment Service Bureau also allowed Kaufman to assist veterans and others in need. An example of his kindnesses followed the time when he was crossing a street in Trenton and was struck by a car. The accident broke his leg. Kaufman neither sued nor pushed for prosecution of the driver but rather, when he discovered that the driver was unemployed, he found the errant man a job. It was also well known within the New Jersey prison system that, upon release, former prisoners could depend on Kaufman to help them find employment to assist in their rehabilitation.

During World War II, Kaufman tried to reenlist in the army but was turned down because of his age and lingering effects from his battle wounds. He later said, "I still regret that they didn't take me because I recovered pretty well and was able to get around with no trouble."

In his later years Kaufman often told the story of when he and other Medal of Honor recipients were invited to the White House by Pres. John F. Kennedy. "He treated us with great reverence at a reception in the Rose Garden probably because he was a veteran himself and knew what we had gone through," he said. Kaufman continued, "He also gave us a personally conducted tour of the White House and showed us many parts that were not generally open to the public."

During the late 1960s, Kaufman, along with other Medal of Honor recipients, actively supported the troops engaged in the Vietnam conflict and spoke out against those protesting the war and its warriors.

In a letter to the Medal of Honor Society on March 19, 1972, Kaufman noted that he had moved from his home at 925 Bellevue Avenue in Trenton to Apartment 34 at 332 W. State Street. He apologized for his handwriting, saying he had been in "ill health, particularly the bursitis in my right arm that makes it rather difficult to grasp a pen." He humorously added that he had no secretary and "I do the best that I can."

Although his health was failing in the last decade of his life, Kaufman still managed, with cane in hand, to take a daily walk around downtown Trenton. In one of his final interviews with the *Asbury Park Press* in 1978, he said, "My only complaint is that I can't see well enough to drive a car these days, and it limits my trips. And I have a special license plate that Governor Byrne gave me."

Kaufman died on February 5, 1981, at the age of eighty-six in Mercer Medical Center in Trenton. His obituary in the *Philadelphia Inquirer* said that he was "the Jewish Sgt. York" and that he was believed to be the last surviving Medal of Honor recipient of World War I. Survivors included his wife, the former Dorothy Finkel; daughter Rita Devries; two grandchildren, and a sister. His is buried Forest Lawn Memorial Park (Section M1, Grave 5) in Trenton.

After his death the Jewish War Veterans Post 156 was renamed in his honor. Kaufman's Medal of Honor is in the collection of the National Museum of American Jewish Military History in Washington, DC.

9

William Sawelson,
World War I, US Army

Company M, 312th Infantry Regiment, 78th Infantry Division

Grandpre, France, October 26, 1918

Date Presented: January 22, 1919

CITATION:

Hearing a wounded man in a shell hole some distance away calling for water, Sgt. Sawelson, upon his own initiative, left shelter and crawled through heavy machine-gun fire to where the man lay, giving him what water he had in his canteen. He then went back to his own shell hole, obtained more water, and was returning to the wounded man when he was killed by a machinegun bullet.

WILLIAM SAWELSON did not kill a large number of Germans, or capture multiple machine-gun positions, or clear trench lines; rather, he earned his medal while bringing comfort to a wounded companion who lay unprotected in "no man's land." He is the only one of the four Jewish American Medal of Honor recipients in World War I to be killed in the conflict. Born on August 5, 1895, in Newark, New Jersey, to Mr. and Mrs. Jacob L. Sawelson, who owned and operated a confectionery store at 618 North 4th Street, he attended local schools in North Newark and high school in nearby Kearney. He resided just north of Newark across the Passac River in Harrison at 315 5th Street when he was inducted into the army on September 8, 1917.

Sawelson joined Company M of the 312th Infantry Regiment, formed from National Guard units in New York and northern Pennsylvania and New Jersey. The 312th had become part of the 78th Infantry Division (Lightning) when it was activated on August 23, 1917, at Camp Dix, New Jersey. During the next eight months, it continued to receive volunteers and draftees as it trained for warfare. In May and June 1918, the division embarked to France, where it continued training before joining the Lorraine Offensive from August 14 through September 7.

On September 12, Sawelson and the 78th Division were "the point of the wedge" in the attack against St. Mihiel that concluded successfully on the 15th. The 78th continued in that role in the final offensive to bring Germany to the Armistice table on September 26 in the Meuse-Argonne Campaign, which ended on November 11.

Sawelson advanced in rank during this period from private to corporal on October 22, 1917, and to sergeant the following July 7. A day after earning his sergeant stripes, his company commander appointed him as the M Company supply sergeant. In that position he no longer fought primarily as a combat infantryman but rather was responsible for securing provisions, ammunition, clothing, and other supplies for his company.

In the war's final offensive, fought at Grandpre on the Aire River just north of the Argonne Forest, Company M became temporarily halted by German machine-gun and artillery fire. Between the American and German lines, a wounded M Company infantryman in a shell hole trapped by cross fire began calling for water. Although, as the unit's supply sergeant, it was not his job to come to the aid of the wounded, Sawelson leaped from his own shell hole and rushed forward amid a hail of machine-gun fire to deliver water to the wounded man. When the soldier emptied Sawelson's canteen, the supply sergeant ran back to his old position, secured more water, and again rushed forward only to fall to machine-gun bullets.

Sawelson was survived by his parents and three siblings. He was only twenty-three years of age; the war was within two weeks of concluding. Sawelson is buried in the Meuse-Argonne American Cemetery and Memorial (Plot C, Row 9, Grave 33) at Romagne, France. He rests under a headstone topped by a large Star of David.

After the Armistice, the 78th Division returned to the United States, where it was demobilized on May 26, 1919. More than a third of its soldiers, 7,144 in total, were casualties—1,169 killed in action, 5,975 wounded in action.

Sawelson's Medal of Honor was presented to his father at a ceremony on Governors Island just off the southern tip of Manhattan on January 22, 1919. He is the only member of the 78th Infantry Division in World War I to be so decorated. Sawelson's medal is currently in the possession of Sawelson's great-nephew Stephen in Palos Verdes, California.

Sgt. William Sawelson VFW Post 340 in Newark is named in his honor. Its original location at 510 N. 5th Street was only a few blocks from the home Sawelson left to be inducted into the US Army.

★★★

10

William Shemin,
World War I, US Army

Company G, 2nd Battalion, 47th Infantry Regiment, 4th Infantry Division
Bazoches, France, August 7–9, 1918
Date Presented: June 2, 2015

CITATION:
Sergeant William Shemin distinguished himself by extraordinary acts of heroism at the risk of his life above and beyond the call of duty while serving as a Rifleman with G Company, 2d Battalion, 47th Infantry Regiment, 4th Division, American Expeditionary Forces, in connection with combat operations against an armed enemy on the Vesle River, near Bazoches, France from August 7 to August 9, 1918. Sergeant Shemin, upon three different occasions, left cover and crossed an open space of 150 yards, repeatedly exposing himself to heavy machine-gun and rifle fire, to rescue wounded. After officers and senior noncommissioned officers had become casualties, Sergeant Shemin took command of the platoon and displayed great initiative under fire until wounded on August 9. Sergeant Shemin's extraordinary heroism and selflessness, above and beyond the call of duty, are in keeping with the highest traditions of the military service and reflect great credit upon himself, with G Company, 2d Battalion, 47th Infantry Regiment.

WILLIAM SHEMIN earned his Medal of Honor as a twenty-year-old infantryman in France. However, it would be ninety-seven years before his valor was formally recognized in a White House ceremony. At the presentation, Pres. Barack Obama said, "We are a nation, a people who remember heroes. We never forget their sacrifice, and we believe that it is never too late to say thank you."

Harris and Bessie Shemin fled the anti-Jewish pogroms in Russia in the late nineteenth century and immigrated to the United States through Ellis Island. They settled in the Bronx, where their son William "Bill" Shemin was born on October 14, 1895. He attended local schools and at age fifteen began playing semi-pro baseball. Shemin then attended the New York State Ranger School (now the State University of New York College of Environmental Science and Forestry Ranger School) in Wanakena, which was established in 1912.

After graduation, according to a US Jewish Servicemen Questionnaire, 1918–1921, compiled by the Office of War Records of the American Jewish Committee, which Shemin completed, he "worked along all different forestry lines doing forest ranger work, followed logging and lumbering in the Adirondacks and Canada. Employed as assistant forester in City of Bayonne." When he registered for the draft on June 5, 1917, he stated that he was living at 14 East 40th Street in Bayonne and that he was natural-born, Caucasian, single, and had no disabilities. His register noted that he was "tall, medium to stocky build, brown eyes, and black hair."

Shermin did not wait to be drafted but rather enlisted in the US Army on October 2, 1917. He reported to Camp Greene, North Carolina, where he underwent basic training and joined Company G, 47th Infantry Regiment, 4th Infantry Division (Ivy) as a rifleman. In May the division moved by rail to Camp Mills on Long Island for embarkation to France. Part of the division was aboard the SS *Megantic* when it was unsuccessfully attacked off the English coast by the German submarine U-43 on May 23.

The 4th Division went ashore at Calais, France, and trained with the British until mid-June at Picardy and then with the French at Meaux before being committed to the front in the Aisne-Marne Offensive on July 28, 1918. Shemin impressed his superiors with his diligence and leadership, earning promotion to corporal on April 20 and to sergeant on June 20. His time in battle would be relatively brief, but it was marked by great valor. After fewer than two weeks of combat, Shermin and the 47th Regiment became heavily engaged with German defenses on August 7, 1918. Three times Shemin rushed into no-man's-land between the trenches amid rifle and machine-gun fire to rescue wounded comrades. Capt. Rupert Purdon, one of Shemin's superiors, later wrote, "With the most utter disregard for his own safety, he sprang from his position in his platoon trench, dashed out across the open in full sight of the Germans, who opened and maintained furious burst of machinegun and rifle fire."

Shemin continued to display valor over the next two days as he "showed great initiative under fire" in taking command of his platoon when his senior leaders became casualties. Despite artillery shrapnel wounds to his legs, he continued to lead the fight until he too fell from a machine-gun round that pierced his helmet and gashed his head. Shemin remained hospitalized for the remainder of the war. A few days after the Armistice, on November 15, 1918, he was awarded the Distinguished Service Cross, the second-highest medal awarded for valor by the United States.

After his release from the medical facility, Shemin rejoined his unit. According to the US Jewish Servicemen Questionnaire, he "served in France and Army of Occupation in Germany and duty in Belgium." The 4th Infantry Division sailed for home in late July 1919, and Shemin was discharged from the service at Camp Merritt, New Jersey, on August 2, 1919.

Shemin worked as a forester at the State Reservation at Niagara Falls, New York, before enrolling in Syracuse University, where he boxed and played football and lacrosse. After graduation in 1924, he moved to the Bronx, where he established a greenhouse and landscaping business, married Bertha Schiffer, and had a son and two daughters. His fourteen grandchildren remember him as being modest about his wartime service. However, he saw to it that they all went through what they called "Shemin basic training": he would wake them each day with orders to "Police the grounds and clean up your areas." They recall him as being short-tempered, tough, and intolerant of slacking and whining. He always emphasized a love for, and obligation to, their country. His daughter, Elsie Shemin-Roth, recalled in a 2015 interview, "My father always said, when our country needs us, we go—no questions asked. Always give more than you're asked."

Shemin was very successful in his nursery business and continued work even after he had to use a cane and had hearing difficulties because of lingering effects from his war wounds. His son Emanuel, or "Manny," joined his father and helped expand the business while also taking time out to serve as an air force lieutenant in the Korean War. Elsie Shemin-Roth's grandson also served four years in the US Marine Corps.

A few days after the 55th anniversary of his valor in France, Shemin died in Greenwich, Connecticut, on August 15, 1973. He is buried in Baron Hirsch Cemetery (Section A, Lot 96, Plot 1) on Staten Island, New York.

Shemin never complained about not receiving the Medal of Honor. In a 2011 interview about her father with the *Kansas City Star*, Shemin-Roth said,

"Being in this war completely changed his life. His whole life was lived differently. He loved this country so much. He was honored to do what he did. He never felt any regret or hostility about what happened."

Some of Shemin's fellow veterans blamed anti-Semitism for Shemin's not receiving the Medal of Honor. Others noted that he had been rapidly promoted despite being a Jew and that the 4th Infantry Division had the reputation of being extremely stingy in awarding medals. In fact, not a single soldier in the 4th Infantry Division was decorated with the Medal of Honor during World War I.

Whatever the reason, Elsie Shemin-Roth always thought her father deserved her country's highest military decoration. In 2001 she read about the pending National Defense Authorization Act that required the military to review Distinguished Service Crosses awarded to Jewish and Hispanic veterans, going back only to World War II, for possible upgrade to the Medal of Honor because of prejudices of the period. She also found a similar bill from 1997 applying to Asian Americans and African Americans.

Shemin-Roth discovered that it would take another "Act of Congress" to authorize a review of her father's Distinguished Service Cross. She soon found an ally in her congressman from her home state of Missouri. Representative Blaine Luetkemeyer introduced the bill in 2010, saying, "It is critically important that we provide brave Jewish Americans like Sgt. Shemin the opportunity to receive the recognition they may not have been afforded because of potential discrimination of the time."

Missouri senators Claire McCaskill and Roy Blunt supported the bill. When it passed and Shemin's DSC was upgraded to the Medal of Honor in 2015, McCaskill said in an Associated Press interview, "Discrimination should never play a role when our country pays tribute to extraordinary acts of courage and selfless sacrifice. I couldn't be prouder that we were able to correct these past injustices, and that William Shemin and other Jewish heroes will get the recognition they deserve, and the national gratitude they earned."

On June 2, 2015, Pres. Barack Obama, surrounded by senior military officers, members of Congress, and family members, presented William Shemin's Medal of Honor posthumously to his daughters Elsie and Ina, both in their eighties. President Obama noted that, on that day in the trenches in France, the soldiers had a terrible choice to make: "Die trying to rescue your fellow soldier or watch him die. William Shemin couldn't stand to watch." The president added that Shemin was "personally utterly fearless."

Elsie Shemin-Roth concluded the ceremony saying, "Discrimination hurts. A wrong has been made right. All is forgiven. This true story could only happen in America. Peace be with each and every one of you. Shalom."

★★★

11

Isadore Seigfried Jachman,
World War II, US Army

Company B, 1st Battalion, 513th Parachute Infantry Regiment,
   17th Airborne Division
Flamierge, Belgium, January 4, 1945
Date Presented: July 25, 1950

CITATION:

For conspicuous gallantry and intrepidity above and beyond the call of duty at Flamierge, Belgium, on 4 January 1945, when his company was pinned down by enemy artillery, mortar, and small arms fire, two hostile tanks attacked the unit, inflicting heavy casualties. S/Sgt. Jachman, seeing the desperate plight of his comrades, left his place of cover and with total disregard for his own safety dashed across open ground through a hail of fire and seizing a bazooka from a fallen comrade advanced on the tanks, which concentrated their fire on him. Firing the weapon alone, he damaged one and forced both to retire. S/Sgt. Jachman's heroic action, in which he suffered fatal wounds, disrupted the entire enemy attack, reflecting the highest credit upon himself and the parachute infantry.

ALTHOUGH HE WAS born in Germany, Isadore S. Jachman volunteered for the US Army after immigrating to the United States. Before he deployed overseas, he told his sister that he wanted to defeat the Nazis and end Hitler's persecution of the Jews.

Born on December 14, 1922, in Berlin to Leo and Lotte Jachman, Isadore's stay in Germany was brief. Leo Jachman, born Leo Jachimowicz, in Kalisz, Poland, had moved to Berlin for better opportunities and then, while Lotte was pregnant with Isadore, he immigrated to the United States. Upon arrival in the new country, he Americanized his name to Jachman and settled in Baltimore on Primrose Avenue where, in August 1923, Lotte and eight-month-old Isadore joined him. Two more children soon joined the family. Leo initially worked as a route salesman for the *Baltimore Sun* and established a grocery business.

The Jachmans continued to practice their Orthodox Jewish faith in America. At age six Isadore (Izzy to his friends and family) entered Baltimore's Yeshiva Torah Ve-Emunah Hebrew Parochial School (now Talmudical Academy of Baltimore), where he studied both Hebrew and secular subjects. At that time, the Hebrew instructors (melamdin) were all elderly men who taught only in Yiddish. This was no problems for Isadore, as he was fluent in the language. After six years at Yeshiva, Jachman graduated on June 25, 1934, and enrolled in PS 40 (Florence Nightingale Junior High School). Each day after his classes at PS 40 Jachman returned to the Yeshiva to continue his Hebrew studies in what was called Yeshiva Chofetz Chaim. He also worked in his father's grocery store at 1510 Ashland Avenue.

Jachman graduated from PS 40 on June 17, 1937, and enrolled in the fall in Baltimore City College High School, known as "The Castle on the Hill" because of its location and architecture, which had been established in 1839. Upon graduation in June 1940 from this public institution, Jachman entered the University of Baltimore, where he remained until he became a soldier. During his high school and college years, Jachman was known as a quiet young man who was popular with his fellow students. He participated in wrestling and weightlifting at the collegiate level as well as at the local Jewish Educational Alliance.

While in college Jachman followed the news about the expanding conflict in Europe through public forums as well as personal letters from family members still living in the war zone who reported the mounting discrimination and harassment of Jews. His concerns were well founded. His father was one of twelve children. One brother was in the French Foreign Legion serving in Morocco. Of the other ten, six would die in Hitler's death camps during the war.

In November 1943, Jachman dropped out of college, enlisted in the US Army, and reported to Fort Riley, Kansas, for basic training. During his training, he so impressed his superiors that he was assigned as a physical fitness instructor after graduation. It did not take long, however, in this position for

Jachman to feel as if he could make more of a contribution to the war effort in some other capacity. He volunteered for Airborne School at Fort Benning, Georgia, and, after training and five parachute jumps, earned the silver wings of a paratrooper.

Jachman then reported to Camp Mackall, North Carolina, where he joined Company B, 1st Battalion, 513th Parachute Infantry, 17th Airborne Division. The 17th Airborne, nicknamed "Thunder from Heaven," had been activated on April 15, 1943. The unit trained in North Carolina and Tennessee until August 17, 1944, when it and Jachman departed for Europe from Camp Miles Standish, Massachusetts. The division landed at Liverpool, England, on August 26 and established its headquarters at Camp Chiseldon near Swindon, where they continued their training, which included low-altitude parachute jumps from 400 feet. Because of his training and leadership skills, Jachman rapidly climbed the ranks to staff sergeant in charge of an infantry squad.

In December the Germans made their surprise offensive in the Ardennes Forest of Belgium, penetrating American lines and creating an intrusion that became known as the Bulge. The 17th Airborne was alerted to reinforce the reeling US units. On December 25–27, the division flew across the English Channel to airstrips and staging areas near Mourmelon, France. They were then transported by trucks to Charleville to assume defensive positions to oppose a possible attack by the Germans across the Meuse River.

On January 1, the 17th Division was reassigned to Gen. George S. Patton's Third Army and ordered to move into Belgium to relieve the battered 28th Infantry Division. General Patton thought the Germans were in full retreat after their unsuccessful attack on Bastogne and ordered the 17th to pursue. Despite terrible weather conditions of snow, fog, and cold—combined with little air and artillery coverage—the 17th advanced. On January 4, 1945, Company B dug in along a roadway on the rear slope that climbed from the village of Monty to Flamierge. Its area would become known as "Dead Man's Ridge" for a reason. The Germans, unfortunately, had not yet given up the fight. In a counterattack supported by artillery and mortars, two Panzer tanks accompanied by infantry attacked B Company. Jackman, despite having only about two weeks in combat, had quickly become a veteran who understood his responsibilities to his men and unit. Just when it appeared that the tanks were going to overrun the Americans' positions, he sprang from his foxhole, grabbed a bazooka from a fallen comrade, and engaged the Panzers. His fire damaged one tank and forced the other to retreat.

The final fire from the tanks struck and killed the Jewish American from Baltimore. Jachman's body, not recovered and identified until almost four months later, was buried in the temporary US Military Cemetery in Foy, Belgium. He was posthumously awarded the Distinguished Service Cross. His body was exhumed and returned home in 1948 and buried in Adath Israel Anshe Sfard Cemetery (Plot 1-8-40) in Dundalk, Maryland.

In 1949, a neighbor of Jachman's father learned about the bravery of his friend's son and wrote to Sen. Herbert R. O'Conor, a former Maryland governor, asking that Isadore's DSC be reviewed for a possible upgrade to the Medal of Honor. The review went all the way to the desk of Pres. Harry Truman, who approved and signed the upgrade on June 9, 1950. On July 25, Lt. Gen. Leonard T. Gerow, commanding general of the Second US Army, presented Jachman's Medal of Honor to his parents in a ceremony at Fort George C. Meade, Maryland.

Jachman's Medal of Honor is in the collection of the National Museum of American Jewish Military History in Washington, DC. On September 19, 1976, the US Army Reserve Center in Owings Mills, Maryland, was dedicated and named in his honor. A drill field at Fort Meade and an athletic facility at Northwestern High School in Baltimore are also named after the Jewish American hero.

12

Ben Louis Salomon,

World War II, US Army

Surgeon, 2nd Battalion, 105th Infantry Regiment, 27th Infantry Division

Saipan, Mariana Islands, July 7, 1944

Date Presented: May 1, 2002

CITATION:

Captain Ben L. Salomon was serving at Saipan, in the Mariana Islands on July 7, 1944, as the Surgeon for the 2d Battalion, 105th Infantry Regiment, 27th Infantry Division. The Regiment's 1st and 2d Battalions were attacked by an overwhelming force estimated between 3,000 and 5,000 Japanese soldiers. It was one of the largest attacks attempted in the Pacific Theater during World War II. Although both units fought furiously, the enemy soon penetrated the Battalions' combined perimeter and inflicted overwhelming casualties. In the first minutes of the attack, approximately 30 wounded soldiers walked, crawled, or were carried into Captain Salomon's aid station, and the small tent soon filled with wounded men. As the perimeter began to be overrun, it became increasingly difficult for Captain Salomon to work on the wounded. He then saw a Japanese soldier bayoneting one of the wounded soldiers lying near the tent. Firing from a squatting position, Captain Salomon quickly killed the enemy soldier. Then, as he turned his attention back to the wounded, two more Japanese soldiers appeared in the front entrance of the tent. As these enemy soldiers were killed, four more crawled under the tent walls. Rushing them, Captain Salomon kicked the knife out of the hand of one, shot another, and bayoneted a third. Captain Salomon butted the fourth enemy soldier in the stomach and a wounded comrade then shot and killed the enemy soldier. Realizing the gravity of the situation, Captain Salomon ordered the wounded to make their way as best they could back to the regimental aid station, while he attempted to hold off the enemy until they were clear. Captain Salomon then grabbed a rifle from one of the wounded and rushed out of the tent. After four men were killed while manning a machine gun, Captain Salomon took control of it. When his body was later found, 98 dead enemy soldiers were piled in front of his position. Captain Salomon's extraordinary heroism and devotion to duty are in keeping with the highest traditions of military service and reflect great credit upon himself, his unit, and the United States Army.

BEN (not Benjamin, as cited in many sources) LOUIS SALOMON is the only US Army dentist to receive the Medal of Honor—and it was not awarded until fifty-eight years after he gave his life fighting to defend his comrades. Born on September 1, 1914, to Kentucky native Ben L. and Bess Leszinsky Salomon in Milwaukee, Wisconsin, the future hero graduated from that city's Shorewood High School. His fellow students remember him as a boy of average height with a bright future who was smart, popular, good-looking, and immaculate in his habits. In all his schooling, Salomon's marks were always at or near the top of his class.

Active in scouting, Salomon advanced to Eagle Scout and enrolled in Marquette University before transferring to the University of Southern California in Los Angeles. Upon earning his undergraduate degree, he entered the USC School of Dentistry and, after graduating in 1937, applied for a commission in the US Army as a dentist. Due to the lack of need for a great number of dentists in the prewar army, his request was turned down.

In 1940, with the need to enlarge the armed forces in response to the expanding war in Europe, Pres. Franklin D. Roosevelt signed the Selective Service Act. Salomon registered for the draft and quickly discovered that the army might not need dentists but was in desperate need of infantrymen. Drafted as an infantry private, Salomon joined the 102nd Infantry Regiment at Fort Ord near Monterey, California, after basic training. He brought along some of his dental tools and during off-duty hours provided teeth cleaning to his fellow soldiers. On some weekends he drove those in the greatest need to his old office in Los Angeles, where he provided free dental care.

Salomon excelled as an infantryman the same way he had in his schooling and in his dental practice. He qualified as Expert with both rifle and pistol and proved to be a natural soldier and leader. His regimental commander stated that Salomon was the "best all-around soldier" in the unit and "the best instructor in infantry we ever had" and that "he gave everybody who ever met him a great lift." The commander concluded, "He had a way of inspiring people to do things that they might not have done otherwise."

Within twelve months, Salomon had earned promotion to sergeant in charge of his company's machine-gun section. It was a skill that he would soon find extremely valuable.

By early 1942 the US. Army's numbers had risen rapidly to meet the challenges of wars on two fronts. The need for dentists also increased, and Salomon was notified that he was to receive an officer's commission and a transfer to the Dental Corps. Salomon attempted to turn down the commission, saying he preferred to remain in the infantry. His commander supported the action and went so far as to try and secure a commission for Salomon as an infantry officer. Neither was successful.

In August 1942, Salomon reported to the 105th Infantry Regiment, 27th Infantry Division (known as the New York Division for its original organization in World War I), at Schofield Barracks, Hawaii, as the regimental dental officer. Some sources have Salomon reporting as late as March of the following year, but the exact date cannot be confirmed. The internal records of the 105th Infantry Regiment were destroyed in combat on Saipan. Salomon's individual records were destroyed in a fire at the National Personnel Records Center in St. Louis, Missouri, in July 1973. As Salomon was an only child, there are no surviving relatives to confirm dates and events.

Salomon approached his duties as regimental dental officer with the same dedication as he had as an infantry sergeant. He was much more than the unit's dentist: he took care of his dental appointments and related duties in the mornings and then joined infantry units in the afternoons to participate in forced marches, range firing, and negotiating obstacle courses.

The 27th Division trained on Hawaii until June 16, 1944, when they and the newly promoted Capt. Salomon went ashore in the invasion of Saipan in the Mariana Islands. When the battalion surgeon of the 2nd Battalion, 105th Regiment, fell wounded from a mortar attack, Salomon, who realized there was little need for a dentist in the midst of combat, volunteered to take his place.

In bloody fighting the 105th pushed the Japanese to the north end of the island. By the night of July 6, the Japanese had run out of room to which to retreat. The Japanese commander issued an order for a final banzai assault, saying, "We will advance to attack the American forces and will all die an honorable death. Each man will kill ten Americans."

The 1st and 2nd Battalions of the 105th anticipated the attack and prepared a joint defensive perimeter in front of the battalion aid stations. Early the next morning, the Japanese counterattacked. A detailed description of Salomon's actions in the later recommendation for the Medal of Honor states:

At dawn on 7 July, the 1st and 2nd Battalions of the 105th Infantry Regiment were attacked by an overwhelming enemy force estimated at between 3,000 and 5,000 Japanese, in one of the greatest mass attacks attempted in the Pacific Theater in World War II. Although both units fought furiously, the enemy soon penetrated their combined perimeter and inflicted overwhelming casualties; any semblance of unit organization and integrity was soon lost. In the first ten minutes of the attack, possibly thirty new wounded walked, crawled, or were carried into the aid station, and the small tent was swarming with men. At one point Captain Salomon stopped work and ordered his assistants to move the less serious cases out under the trees to make room to work on the more grievously wounded. As the outer perimeter began to be overrun and more wounded drifted back, it became increasingly difficult for him to work. Soon his ministrations were interrupted by the sight of a Japanese soldier bayoneting one of the wounded, lying near the seaward tent wall. Firing from a squatting position, he quickly killed the enemy. No sooner had he turned back to the wounded than two more Japanese appeared in the front entrance of the tent. By the time these were shot, clubbed, and bayoneted, four more came crawling under the tent walls. Rushing over to them, he kicked the knife out of the hand of one, shot another, and bayoneted the third. The fourth was shot by one of the wounded from his stretcher after Captain Salomon had butted him in the stomach as he lunged across the room to retrieve the knife with which he stabbed its owner to death. Realizing the gravity of the situation, he ordered the wounded to make their way as best they could back to the regimental aid station, while he attempted to hold off the enemy until they were clear. He knew that the Japanese killed wounded men without mercy, and shared his fellow soldier's strong reluctance to leave wounded comrades where they might fall victims to the enemy. He then grabbed a rifle from one of the wounded, and rushed out of the tent. He was seen once in a kneeling position, firing his rifle. Later, after four men had been killed on one machinegun, one right after another, Captain Salomon took it over. When his body was found, it was still slumped over the machinegun. Ninety-eight Japanese bodies were piled in front of his gun position. From the pattern in which the bodies lay, it was obvious that he had moved the gun four different times as the bodies piled high in front of it to get a new field of fire. The seventy-six bullet holes in his body, twenty-four of which were sustained before he died, told the story of the pain and suffering he endured. The crude bayonet wounds which his body bore were mute testimony to the savagery of the enemy and the sacrifice he made that this might not happen to the wounded soldiers for whose welfare and protection he had taken responsibility. Captain Salomon's heroic action allowed an untold number of wounded to retire to safety.

Witnesses later recalled that Salomon's last words were shouts to his fellow soldiers who were evacuating the wounded. He said, "I'll hold them off until you get them to safety. See you later."

No American saw him alive again. Captain Salomon's remains were returned to the United States, where his ashes are interred in Glendale, California, at Forest Lawn Memorial Park in the Great Mausoleum, Columbarium of Guidance (Iris Terrace Section, Lot 0, Space 21994). The ashes of his mother, who died in 1946, and his father, who passed in 1970, are in the same space.

Cremation is not explicitly prohibited by Jewish law; however, there are prohibitions on defiling dead bodies and there are detailed procedures for handling remains prior to burial. The reasons for Salomon's parents electing cremation for themselves and their son are unknown, especially because cremation brings images of the mass burnings of corpses of Jews by the Germans during the Holocaust.

Much of what we know about the battle on Saipan, where Salomon gave his life defending his patients, comes from the research of Capt. Edmund G. Love. As the historian of the 27th Division, he walked the battlefield soon after the fight concluded, interviewed many of the survivors of the battle, and prepared Medal of Honor recommendations for Salomon as well as Lt. Col. William J. O'Brien, the commander of the 1st Battalion, 105th Infantry Regiment, and Sgt. Thomas A. Baker of the battalion's Company A. Many of Love's findings were later published in his book *War Is a Private Affair*.

Love briefly left the 27th Division for other duties but returned in April 1945 to provide historical coverage of the Battle of Okinawa. When he checked on the Medal of Honor recommendations he had submitted, he discovered that those for O'Brien and Baker had been approved but that Salomon's had been returned with a brief hand written note from Maj. Gen. George W. Grinder, the commanding general of the 27th Division. Grinder wrote, "I am deeply sorry that I cannot approve the award of this medal to Captain Salomon, although he richly deserves it. At the time of his death, this officer was in the medical service and wore a Red Cross brassard upon his arm. Under the rules of the Geneva Convention, to which the United States subscribes, no medical officer can bear arms against the enemy."

Love attempted with no success to get Grinder to change his mind or to secure the support of other officers in the 105th Regiment. Grinder stood by his original decision and, unfortunately, most of the regimental officers had become casualties and were no longer available.

After the war, Love joined the Office of the Chief of Military History in Washington, DC, as a civilian historian with the responsibility for writing about various battles in the Pacific. In 1946 he wrote an article for the *Infantry Journal* about the Battle of Saipan that included the story of Ben Salomon. Salomon's father knew nothing of the circumstance of his son's death and his battlefield valor until he heard Love's story read over the radio. In fact, the elder Salomon had received only a basic telegram about his son's death. He did not even receive a posthumous Purple Heart for his son, let alone any notification about a Medal of Honor nomination. He wrote a letter to Sec. of War Robert Patterson asking for details.

It was a wise action on the part of the elder Salomon. Patterson, a former New York attorney and district judge, had served in World War I as a major and had earned the Distinguished Service Cross and Silver Star with the 77th Infantry Division in France. Patterson not only directed Love to brief the elder Salomon with details on his son's death but also ordered him to prepare a new recommendation for a Medal of Honor.

Love easily fulfilled the first part of his instructions from Patterson. He flew to Los Angeles and personally briefed Salomon about his son's valor. Preparing the new award decoration recommendation was not so easy. The original award paperwork could not be found, and most of Love's notes about the period had been filed and lost by the Office of the Adjutant General. Further complicating the process was that few of the witnesses to the battle had survived the war, nor could the living be located since their discharge. Love finally located Maj. Edward McCarthy, who had commanded the 2nd Battalion, 105th Infantry, on Saipan.

It was not until the summer of 1951 that Love, using statements from McCarthy and witnesses he had been able to identify, completed the recommendation and submitted it through the Office of the Chief of Military History. By then Patterson was no longer the head of what was now the Department of Defense and no one at that level championed the recommendation. It was returned without further action with the explanation that the time limit had expired for the submission of World War II awards. Love left government service to become a successful writer of twenty books, including *Subways Are for Sleeping*, which was adapted into a successful Broadway musical.

No further action was taken until the late 1960s, when Dr. John I. Ingle, dean of the USC School of Dentistry, heard from his friend, the elder Salomon, the story of Ben Salomon's valor and the fact that it had not been formally recognized. In 1968, Ingle contacted Maj. Gen. Robert B. Shira, chief of the Army Dental Corps, and urged him to reopen the investigation into securing an award for Salomon. It would be a difficult task. Neither of the previous award recommendations could be found and Major McCarthy was deceased. Ingle and Shira called upon Edmond Love for assistance, and the former captain once again wrote about what he had seen and uncovered in his previous investigations. Love attended a reunion of veterans of the 27th Infantry Division and located another witness that led to correspondence with yet other veterans who had seen the aftermath of the battle and the numerous bodies around Salomon's machine-gun position.

Research efforts were bolstered by the passage of congressional legislation in 1960 that removed the legal time restrictions on submissions of awards for actions in World War II. Love completed the recommendation, and on October 29, 1969, the surgeon general of the US Army, Lt. Gen. Hal B. Jennings, signed what was the third Medal of Honor recommendation for Salomon. The Office of the Judge Advocate General reviewed the recommendation and stated that the original interpretation of the statues of the 1929 Geneva Convention that prevented medical personnel from receiving valor awards for fighting was not valid. The JAG finding stated that medical personnel were allowed to bear arms in self-defense and during efforts to protect the wounded and sick.

With the two hurdles of time limitation and the Geneva Convention now eliminated, the recommendation was approved by the Senior Army Decorations Board and by the Joint Chiefs of Staff. Stanley R. Resor, the secretary of the army, recommended approval and forwarded the request to Sec. of Defense Melvin R. Laird on July 21, 1970. The Office of the Secretary of Defense did not look favorably on the action, citing legal matters that had already been settled but nonetheless calling for further investigation. It took nearly two years for the various legal councils to once again find that Salomon was eligible for the Medal of Honor. Once more, however, the request was re-turned to the army for further review. On March 28, 1972, the new secretary of the army, Robert F. Froehlke, again forwarded the request to Laird, stat-ing, "After careful review of the 1944 Medal of Honor case involving Captain Ben Salomon, I'm convinced that the Army is absolutely right in trying to redress a 27-year-old error of judgement. The case has been painstakingly reconstructed. It has been endorsed unanimously for approval by the Army Senior Decorations Board and the Joint Chiefs of Staff, and my predecessor, Stan Resor . . . this one deserves to be approved."

Despite the efforts and support of many, Ben Salomon was not yet to re-ceive the medal that he so richly deserved. On June 10, 1972, the Office of the Secretary of Defense returned the recommendation to the army with-out approval, stating that it was based on circumstantial evidence. Although there is no conclusive evidence, there may have been political reasons for not approving the award. Some thought that the White House of Pres. Richard Nixon was concerned about straining relations with Japan by bringing up unpleasant memories of World War II. Relations between the two former belligerents were all that more important because Japan was concerned about the ongoing efforts by the United States to establish diplomatic relations with Communist China.

While the Department of Defense failed to recognize Salomon's valor, he was not forgotten. The USC School of Dentistry named a clinic in his honor in the 1960s and, in 1972, a dental clinic at Fort Benning, Georgia, was dedicated in his memory.

Other than these two minor events, the story of Salomon's day of valor re-mained dormant over the next two decades. It was not until the mid-1990s that army dentist Col. John E. King, while researching the history of the Dental Corps during the war in Vietnam, learned about Salomon's actions. About the same time, Dr. Robert West, a veteran of World War II and a graduate of the USC School of Dentistry, began work on a history of the institution for a book to commemorate the upcoming 100th anniversary of the school.

West coordinated with Dr. Ingle to learn about the previous efforts to se-cure Salomon the decoration. Ingle provided his contacts, which led to West and King's meeting. King made available the paperwork from the 1969 efforts to West, who said in a later interview, published in the *Journal of the California Dental Association*, "This was an error in the history of our nation. I became obsessed. It had to be fixed."

When West had gathered all the appropriate paperwork, he began a letter-writing campaign to the Senior Army Decorations Board, the chief of the Army Dental Corps, and the Office of the Secretary of the Army. He also enlisted the assistance of California congressman Brad Sherman. In his letter to the congressman, written on July 7, 1997—the 53rd anniversary of Salomon's fight on Saipan—West concluded, "The Alumni Association of the USC School of Dentistry implores you to correct this wrong! Dr. Ben Salomon is a true American hero . . . And 53 years later, it is not too late to correct this wrong! Give Ben his medal!"

Salomon's paperwork moved slowly through the system with West, the deputy surgeon general of the United States, and the chief of the Army Dental Corps closely monitoring its progress. It finally achieved approval from both the Department of the Army and the Department of Defense, after which Congressman Sherman sponsored legislation as a part of the 2002 Defense Authorization Act that finally secured the Medal of Honor for the Jewish dentist.

Dr. West later said, "I never once thought of giving up. What stuck with me was the fact that, when Capt. Ben Salomon left that tent, he must have known he was going to die, and yet he never hesitated. He was a true hero."

On May 1, 2002, Pres. George W. Bush presented Salomon's Medal of Honor to Dr. West in a White House ceremony in the Rose Garden. No direct family members were still alive, and his "dentist family" agreed that the West, fellow alumnus of Salomon at the USC School of Dentistry, was the one to receive the medal. Also receiving the Medal of Honor in the same ceremony was the widow of Capt. Jon E. Swanson, an army helicopter pilot who died supporting South Vietnamese soldiers in a battle in Cambodia in 1971.

Before the presentation of Salomon's medal, President Bush noted that none of the dentist's living relatives were present but that America would always know of the bravery of Captain Salomon, whose Medal of Honor citation "tells of one young man who was the match for one hundred, a person of true valor."

President Bush concluded the ceremony by saying, "These two events we recognize today took place a generation apart, but they represent the same tradition. That tradition of military valor and sacrifice has preserved our country, and continues to this day. Captain Salomon and Captain Swanson never lived to wear this medal, but they will be honored forever in the memory of our country."

After the presentation, West gave the medal to the US Army Medical Department Museum at Fort Sam Houston in San Antonio, Texas. A duplicate of the medal is on display at the USC School of Dentistry in Los Angeles.

Edmond Love also provided an appropriate tribute to Salomon in *War Is a Private Affair*. Voicing his support for a Medal of Honor for Salomon, Love wrote, "During the war in the Pacific, as a historian, in seven battles with four divisions, I studied the individual actions of thousands of men. I personally prepared, at the request of various division and regimental commanders, the papers which resulted in the award of seven Congressional Medals of Honors and countless other decorations. I do not know of a man more richly deserving of this high honor than Captain Salomon."

13

Raymond Zussman,
World War II, US Army

Company A, 756th Tank Battalion, 3rd Infantry Division
Noroy-le-Bourg, France, September 12, 1944
Date Presented: May 24, 1945

CITATION:

On 12 September 1944, 2d Lt. Zussman was in command of two tanks operating with an infantry company in the attack on enemy forces occupying the town of Noroy-le-bourg, France. At 7:00 P.M., his command tank bogged down. Throughout the ensuing action, armed only with a carbine, he reconnoitered alone on foot far in advance of his remaining tank and the infantry. Returning only from time to time to designate targets, he directed the action of the tank and turned over to the infantry the numerous German soldiers he had caused to surrender. He located a road block and directed his tanks to destroy it. Fully exposed to fire from enemy positions only 50 yards distant, he stood by his tank directing its fire. Three Germans were killed and eight surrendered. Again he walked before his tank, leading it against an enemy-held group of houses, machine-gun and small-arms fire kicking up dust at his feet. The tank fire broke the resistance and 20 enemy surrendered. Going forward again alone he passed an enemy-occupied house from which Germans fired on him and threw grenades in his path. After a brief firefight, he signaled his tank to come up and fire on the house. Eleven German soldiers were killed and 15 surrendered. Going on alone, he disappeared around a street corner. The fire of his carbine could be heard and in a few minutes he reappeared driving 30 prisoners before him. Under 2d Lt. Zussman's heroic and inspiring leadership, 18 enemy soldiers were killed and 92 captured.

AT THE MEDAL OF HONOR presentation ceremony for his son, Nathan Zussman said, "My son, Ray, died just as he always lived, fighting for what he felt was right and just." Raymond was born on July 23, 1917, to Nathan and Rebecca Leah Raymound Zussman at their home at 9144 Joseph Campau in Hamtramck, Michigan, a northeastern suburb of Detroit. His mother, born in Lithuania, gave birth to eight children—four boys and four girls. As a boy, Ray worked in his father's shoe store and sang in his synagogue's choir. "Ray," as he was called by friends, came from a family of proud veterans of military service. The senior Zussman had been a soldier in Czarist Russia and fought in the Russo-Japanese War in 1904–1905. His eldest brother, Abraham, was a US Army veteran of World War I and had been wounded in action while serving as a captain.

Zussman attended Durfee Elementary and Intermediate Schools, which had been established in 1927 to educate the growing population of children of recent working-class European immigrants. Among this group was what the school's history notes as "a sizable number of Jewish students." Zussman then attended Detroit's Central High School, where, despite his size of only five feet four inches tall and weighing 140 pounds, he tried out for the football team. He also participated in basketball, tennis, and track. Friends described him as broad-shouldered, fair-haired, intelligent, and good-natured. They said he was always willing to accept a challenge.

Upon graduation, Zussman joined Teamsters Local 337 in Detroit and quickly rose to the position of shop steward. He also enrolled in night classes at Wayne State University and studied metallurgy at the Detroit Institute of Technology.

Zussman was drafted into the US Army on September 24, 1941, and completed basic training at Fort Sill, Oklahoma, before reporting to Fort Knox, Kentucky. At Fort Knox, he trained in tank operations and tactics and then acted as an instructor in the same training. He graduated from Armored Officers Candidate School on January 9, 1943, and shipped out to Africa the following June to join the 756th Tank Battalion. The 756th went ashore in Italy at Salerno attached to the 3rd Infantry Division on September 17. In early 1944, Zussman was wounded during the Battle of Monte Cassino in Italy and was evacuated to a rear area hospital. When he recovered, he was offered a headquarters assignment, but Zussman refused and asked to be returned to a combat position. Back with the 756th as a platoon leader of M-4 Sherman tanks, Zussman landed near St. Tropez, France, on August 15, 1944, as a part of Operation Dragoon and began the push up the Rhone Valley.

On September, 12, 1944, at 1900 hours, Lt. Zussman was in command of a tank section supporting an infantry company at Noroy-le-Bourg. *The History of the Third Infantry Division in World War II* expands on the citation for the Medal of Honor earned by Zussman. It states,

> Lieutenant Zussman dismounted from his command tank and proceeded on foot, armed only with a carbine and followed by a lone M-4 tank, and assaulted Noroy-le-Bourg, France. Forging ahead on the tank into blazing small-arms fire, he located and neutralized an improvised roadblock which had been booby trapped. Although intense enemy machine-gun and small-arms fire from a German position only 50 yards distant ricocheted off the hull and turret of the tank, Lieutenant Zussman stood beside it, fully exposed, firing on the enemy with his carbine and directing the tank's fire. When three Germans fell dead, the remaining eight surrendered to Lieutenant Zussman, who immediately proceeded to direct the fire of the tank on another center of resistance, killing three and compelling an additional seven to surrender. Having already exhausted his carbine ammunition, he seized a Thompson submachine gun from a member of the tank crew and advanced well in front of the tank, toward a group of houses occupied by the enemy. Machine-gun and small-arms fire opened up on him from another enemy strongpoint 75 yards to his right front. Disregarding bullets which kicked up the dirt at his feet, he again stood in an exposed position and directed the fire of his tank until resistance was broken and 20 Germans surrendered. Leaving the tank behind, he rushed toward and enemy strongpoint in a house, firing his submachine gun as he ran, while the Germans tried to stop him with small-arms fire and threw hand grenades in his path. After a brief fire exchange, he brought up the tank and directed its fire on the house, forcing 11 more Germans to give up. His submachine gun blazing, Lieutenant Zussman again dashed forward into rifle and automatic weapons fire to another German-held house, emerging after a short exchange of fire with 15 more prisoners. As the Germans fled before his whirlwind attack accurate tank fire accounted for 11 more killed. Noting an ideal antitank position, he plunged forward alone to reconnoiter. His submachine gun fired; his voice was heard above the tumult, shouting *"Hände hoch!"* and in a few minutes 30 prisoners, including the crews of two AT guns, filed around the corner. As night fell, he again went forward alone, to a truck; there was a hand grenade explosion, but when the smoke cleared

Lieutenant Zussman returned with another prisoner. With lightning rapidity, Lieutenant Zussman had overwhelmed one enemy position after another. Fighting against all odds and on his own volition, he had blasted his way into and through the strongly defended town ahead of the infantry, killing 17 and capturing 92 soldiers, and capturing 2 antitank guns, one 20mm flak gun, two machine guns, and two trucks.

With the way secured, Zussman's unit continued the attack. Nine days later, on September 21, he was killed by a German mortar blast. On June 9, 1945, Maj. Gen. Charles L. Scott, the commanding general of the Armored Center at Fort Knox, presented Nathan Zussman his son's Medal of Honor at the 75th graduation exercise of the Officers Candidate School. After receiving the medal, the senior Zussman said,

> It is indeed with great pride that I appear before this graduating class, for several years ago, I too, had a son who was commissioned in this same training center, and I looked to him with great pride just as your parents are looking forward to you and your accomplishments. A pride to think that you have a son duly qualified to take his just place with our Armed Forces, for a country which they are so devoted to, for the protection of the rights which our people stand for. While I have come here with great pride, I still come with a heavy heart, having given a son for the freedom which I sought, years ago having left a country where the people were oppressed by the yokes of oppression and prejudice, and sought freedom and liberty, which I have enjoyed in this country for the past 45 years. During the 45 years that I have enjoyed the freedom and liberty of this Country, it has made me indeed grateful and proud to think that I have been able to give a son to this great cause that he, my son, in his indomitable courage and with the thought ever in his mind of my leaving a country of oppression, to seek the freedom of this country—fought to preserve them and was awarded the highest honors that could be bestowed by this, our country, for his bravery in action.

Raymond was initially buried in France but was brought home and laid to final rest on June 6, 1949, in the Veterans Section of Machpelah Cemetery (Section 6, Row 15, Lot 17, Grave 298) in Ferndale, Michigan. Zussman's family requested a simple Jewish funeral but, at the insistence of the Detroit Jewish Veterans Re-burial Committee, allowed the casket to lie in state in the main sanctuary at Congregation Shaarey Zedek in the Detroit suburb of Southfield. An honor guard flanked the casket, and full military honors were rendered at the cemetery. The family turned down the offer from the military for a caisson with escort and a request from the City of Detroit for the body to lie in state at city hall.

Zussman made an impression on more than just his family and friends. In his last conversation with his father before going overseas, the newly commission lieutenant said, "You look after Rags (his puppy sheepdog). He's my pal and he's going to be a great dog." Six years later, and four years after his death, popular Detroit artist Benjamin Glicker painted a memorial portrait of Zussman. When it was exhibited at the family home, Rags ran to the picture, lay down next to it, and did not move for the remainder of the day.

The Lt. Raymond Zussman Jewish War Veterans Post 333 in Oak Park, Michigan, is named in his honor, as is a playground in Detroit and a park in Hamtramck. In 1944, the US Army launched the *Lt. Raymond Zussman (FS-246)*. It was later transferred to the US Fish and Wildlife Service until it was taken out of service in 1963. In 2000 the army dedicated Zussman Village at Fort Knox for training in urban terrain. Photographs and documents from Zussman's life are in the collection of the Rabbi Leo M. Franklin Archives in Temple Beth El in Bloomfield Hills, Michigan.

★★★

14

Tibor Rubin,

Korea, US Army

Company I, 8th Cavalry Regiment, 1st Cavalry Division

Korea, July 23, 1950–April 20, 1953

Date Presented: September 23, 2005

CITATION:

For conspicuous gallantry and intrepidity at the risk of his life above and beyond the call of duty: Corporal Tibor Rubin distinguished himself by extraordinary heroism during the period from July 23, 1950, to April 20, 1953, while serving as a rifleman with Company I, 8th Cavalry Regiment, 1st Cavalry Division. While his unit was retreating to the Pusan Perimeter, Corporal Rubin was assigned to stay behind to keep open the vital Taegu-Pusan Road link used by his withdrawing unit. During the ensuing battle, overwhelming numbers of North Korean troops assaulted a hill defended solely by Corporal Rubin. He inflicted a staggering number of casualties on the attacking force during his personal 24-hour battle, single-handedly slowing the enemy advance and allowing the 8th Cavalry Regiment to complete its withdrawal successfully. Following the breakout from the Pusan Perimeter, the 8th Cavalry Regiment proceeded northward and advanced into North Korea. During the advance, he helped capture several hundred North Korean soldiers. On October 30, 1950, Chinese forces attacked his unit at Unsan, North Korea, during a massive nighttime assault. That night and throughout the next day, he manned a .30 caliber machine gun at the south end of the unit's line after three previous gunners became casualties. He continued to man his machine gun until his ammunition was exhausted. His determined stand slowed the pace of the enemy advance in his sector, permitting the remnants of his unit to retreat south-

ward. As the battle raged, Corporal Rubin was severely wounded and captured by the Chinese. Choosing to remain in the prison camp despite offers from the Chinese to return him to his native Hungary, Corporal Rubin disregarded his own personal safety and immediately began sneaking out of the camp at night in search of food for his comrades. Breaking into enemy food storehouses and gardens, he risked certain torture or death if caught. Corporal Rubin provided not only food to the starving Soldiers, but also desperately needed medical care and moral support for the sick and wounded of the POW camp. His brave, selfless efforts were directly attributed to saving the lives of as many as forty of his fellow prisoners. Corporal Rubin's gallant actions in close contact with the enemy and unyielding courage and bravery while a prisoner of war are in the highest traditions of military service and reflect great credit upon himself and the United States Army.

TIBOR RUBIN survived the Nazi concentration camps as a teenager, immigrated to the United States after the war where he volunteered for the army, earned his Medal of Honor by single-handedly holding a hill against an enemy attack, and was captured and kept prisoner by the Chinese for two and a half years. It then took more than a half century before his medal was approved and awarded.

Rubin was born on June 18, 1929, in Paszto, Hungary. His father, Ferenc, a shoemaker, fought in the Hungarian army during World War I and had been captured by the Russians and kept prisoner in Siberia for six years. He was a strict disciplinarian who demanded Tibor and his brothers and sisters continue their Jewish religious training and traditions while also insisting they mix with and respect their non-Jewish neighbors. Tibor's mother, who bore four children with Ferenc, died of cancer when he was a baby. The mother Tibor knew and loved was actually his stepmother, Rosa. As a boy, Tibor skipped Jewish classes and did not take his religion seriously. This drew criticism from his father, but his stepmother was much more forgiving and helped Tibor set up a local delivery service. Tips from his deliveries gave Tibor a sense of independence and paid his admission to the local movie house where he leaned about, and fell in love with, the United States through watching American films.

When the Nazis began rounding up Hungarian Jews in 1944 for the death camps, the Rubins sent Tibor on a long foot march to neutral Switzerland. German sentries, however, stopped Tibor at the Swiss border in early April and sent him to the concentration camp at the hilltop fortress in Mauthausen,

Austria. At the camp Rubin learned to survive the harsh working conditions and to avoid the gas chambers to live as a self-described "rat." He kept a low profile and sneaked out of his barracks at night to pilfer the German kitchens for himself and his fellow Jewish prisoners.

Rubin endured more than a year in the camp before the US Army's 11th Armored Division liberated Mauthausen on May 5, 1945. Although the Nazis destroyed most of the camp's records, it is estimated that 150,000 to 200,000 perished within its walls and outlying camps. Rubin's father died in Buchenwald. His sister Edith disappeared into one of the death camps. Rosa Rubin and two of Tibor's sisters, Irene and Ilonka, were sent to Auschwitz. During their processing into the camp, the ten-year-old Ilonka was separated and put into the line headed for the gas chambers. Rosa, who had been directed to the labor line, ran to join her youngest child. She yelled to Irene, who survived the war, "I'll go with Ilonka; she should not have to die alone."

With assistance from the Red Cross, Tibor reunited with his two brothers and Irene in the summer of 1945 at the displaced persons camp at Pocking in Bavaria, Germany, near the border with Austria. During his time in the camp, Tibor later recalled that he did little but learn to play Ping-Pong and to be thoroughly repulsed by the Spam provided in their rations. After a year, Tibor, still only fifteen years old, transferred to a children's camp two hours west at Landshut, Germany.

After six months at Landshut, a letter from an uncle in New York offered Tibor a place to live and a visa sponsorship. With assistance from JOINT, a Jewish charity that aided refugees, he secured immigration papers and a berth aboard the SS *Marine Flasher* and sailed to America. An article in *Time* magazine at the time described the aging ocean liner as a floating flophouse with too few toilets and cramped staterooms. Tibor, however, thought the ship was wonderful and was greatly impressed with the quality and amount of food. He later claimed to have been the first in line and the last to leave the dining hall for every meal.

Rubin arrived in New York City on May 26, 1948. Despite not speaking English, he immediately found work as a busboy in a restaurant and then moved on to a better-paying job in a clothing factory. As with many Medal of Honor recipients, some of their backgrounds are recorded incorrectly. Such is the instance of Rubin's second job in New York. Nearly every account states that Rubin worked in a shoe factory or as a shoemaker. It is fortunate that Rubin worked closely with his biographer, Daniel M. Cohen, for his 2015 book, *Single Handed*. According to the book, Rubin worked in a garment factory where cloth was cut and sewed. The confusion likely comes from Rubin dating a young woman who worked in a shoe factory next to his place of employment.

From the clothing factory, he went to work in a slaughterhouse, where at times he had to cut and process pork. Rubin, who mostly kept kosher, did not complain and looked at it as "work is work." He remained a butcher for a few months before an upscale Jewish-owned grocery store on Broadway hired him to assist customers.

"Ted," as he was now called, enjoyed living and working in New York but felt that he owed something to his adopted country. To a friend he said, "Ever since the army saved me from the Nazis, I promised myself to pay them back." Twice he attempted to enlist, only to be turned down because of his limited English skills. When a family friend who owned a large scrap-metal business in Oakland, California, offered Ted a job, he bought a cross-country bus ticket and headed west in the fall of 1949.

After six months of working in construction, Rubin, for the third time, attempted to join the army in the spring of 1950. The recruiter at the Oakland station listened to Rubin's story of previous attempts to enlist and then sat him between a navy veteran and a marine veteran who were testing to join the army. With a little help from his new friends he easily passed the test. Although the recruiter discussed butcher school and even language training, Rubin was not surprised to be assigned to the infantry.

Rubin did his basic training at Fort Ord, California, where he excelled in physical tests and marksmanship. With his experiences in the concentration camps, he had no trouble with the discipline and especially liked the "three hots and a cot" (three meals a day and a bunk) that the army provided. On completion of his training, Rubin joined 4,500 other recruits aboard the USS *General Nelson M. Walker* en route to the island of Okinawa.

More infantry training followed on Okinawa. When North Korea invaded South Korea on June 25, 1950, Rubin was assigned to Company I, 8th Cavalry Regiment of the 1st Cavalry Division. The 1st Cavalry went ashore at P'ohang-dong near the southern end of South Korea on July 18, 1950, and almost immediately went into combat against the North Koreans.

Rubin got along well with his fellow soldiers, who were mostly from southern states and who had had little contact with Jews. His 1st sergeant was a different matter. He was anti-Semitic and often expressed his hatred of Jews.

When there was a difficult task or mission, the sergeant often shouted, "Get me that fucking Jew," or "Where is that Hungarian son-of-a-bitchin' Jew?"

Soon after they landed, the 1st Cavalry struggled to stop the North Koreas from pushing them off the peninsula as they retreated into the Pusan Perimeter. In one fight, the racist sergeant ordered Rubin to defend a hill single-handedly while the rest of the company withdrew. Rubin remained alone on the hill as he killed many and turned the others back. When he rejoined his unit, his company commander, according to Rubin's biography, told the 1st sergeant, "Tibor Rubin is recommended for the Medal of Honor for distinguishing himself conspicuously by gallantry, at the risk of his life above and beyond the call of duty, to kill hundreds of enemy soldiers, stopping their advance" and "securing the only road from Taegu to Pusan, saving the lives of countless soldiers of our and our allies, so that our only main road will be open at least for the next twenty-four hours."

Several of Rubin's fellow soldiers witnessed the company commander's remarks. However, the company commander was killed in action three days later, and the 1st sergeant never submitted the paperwork for the medal. Instead, he continued to send Rubin on patrols and other dangerous duties.

The North Koreans made another all-out attack on the Pusan Perimeter in early September. A mortar round landed near Rubin, driving shrapnel into his right leg from knee to ankle. Medics transported him to a field hospital where doctors determined that he should be evacuated to Japan or the States for treatment. Rubin refused, and as soon as he could walk on his own, he reported back to Company I. The 1st sergeant immediately put him back on patrol and guard duty.

On September 15, the Allies made an amphibious landing at Inchon on the northwest coast of South Korea. The Americans in the Pusan Perimeter launched a counterattack at the same time that began driving the enemy northward. Along the way, Rubin exposed himself to enemy fire to rescue a wounded soldier and then, while on patrol, encountered an entire North Korean regiment seeking to surrender. Single-handedly he marched the prisoners to the rear. He was once again recommended for medals, but again, because of the bias of the 1st sergeant and the death of the new company commander, no action was taken.

By the end of October, the 8th Cavalry Regiment had crossed the 38th Parallel into North Korea and continued its offensive to within fifty miles of the Chinese border. There were rumors that the soldiers would be back in the States for Christmas. That did not happen. On October 30, the three battalions of the 8th Cavalry established defenses around the town of Unsan near Camel's Head Bend of the Nammyon River. Two days later a massive Chinese army, which had entered the war on the side of their fellow North Korean communists, attacked en masse. Greatly outnumbered, the 8th Cavalry began a withdrawal of two battalions, with the third battalion left in place to cover the retreat.

Rubin and the rest of Company I took the brunt of the attack. He manned a machine gun that covered the primary approach to his company's position and held out until a hand grenade destroyed his gun and ripped shrapnel into his hand, chest, and leg. Rubin staggered to the rear and joined the survivors of his company. His remaining officers said that he would receive a Silver Star for his actions, but it was forgotten in the turmoil of the remaining fight.

On November 3 the survivors attempted to break out to friendly lines to the south. Some made it; many did not. Back in the perimeter at Unsan, the battalion surgeon and chaplain of the 8th Cavalry's 3rd Battalion gathered the wounded, including Rubin, who could not be evacuated, and prepared to surrender. After their capture, the Americans were marched northward. Those not seriously wounded helped those who were more seriously injured. If a man could not keep up, he was shot. Rubin would be listed as Missing in Action until the army finally verified his status as a POW and notified his family on December 20, 1951.

Despite his wounds from the hand grenade and the earlier leg wound that still had not healed, Rubin helped carry those who could not walk and treated their wounds the best he could under the circumstances. He continued to help his fellow prisoners at their first temporary camp, called Death Valley, where they stayed for two months, and later at Camp 5, where they lived for more than two years.

During his captivity, Rubin endured cold, hunger, and harsh treatment from his guards, threats of execution, and constant propaganda. He not only survived but also renewed his skills that he had learned in the Nazi concentration camp of pilfering of food for his fellow prisoners and caring for them the best he could. When asked how he endured, he replied that the POW camp was "a piece of cake" compared to what he had suffered under the Nazis.

Pres. George W. Bush later said of Rubin's actions in the POW camp,

Those who served with Ted speak of him as a soldier whose many acts of compassion helped his fellow GIs survive the nightmare of imprisonment. As a teenager, Ted had taught himself how to survive the horrors of a Nazi death camp. He was resourceful, courageous, and unusually strong. And in Korea, he drew on these qualities to help keep many of his POWs alive. Whenever he could, at the risk of certain execution, Corporal Rubin would sneak out and steal food rations from the guards, and then he shared them with his fellow soldiers. Throughout this ordeal he nursed those who were sick back to health, and said the Kaddish prayers for those he buried.

Fellow POW Leo Cormier later wrote, "He shared his food evenly among the GIs. He nursed us and did many good deeds. He told us that as a Jew, helping his fellow man was the most important thing to him."

When the Chinese discovered Rubin's national origin, they offered to send him back to their fellow communist country. Rubin refused, as he recognized it as a propaganda ploy and had no desire to go back to Hungary. He also felt an obligation to stay with his fellow soldiers.

During the negotiations for a truce in the spring of 1953, the two sides began a prisoner exchange. Rubin, likely because his original leg wound was becoming worse, was one of the first exchanged in what was called Little Switch. On April 22, Rubin sent his brother, who had immigrated to Long Beach, California, a telegram: "Dear Brother. Arrived safely. Am in good army hospital. Never so happy to be an American as today. Am anxiously awaiting the time when I'll be home with you. Hope you received word of my return from prison camp. Regards to everyone."

Before Rubin left the POW camp, he made a list of all the prisoners who were not yet to be released. He hid the list in the bandages around his leg and turned it over to American officials at his first hospital in Seoul. After a series of hospitalizations in Japan and Hawaii, Rubin finally made it to California on May 5, 1953. The *Long Beach Herald-Express* carried a picture of Rubin and his brother celebrating his return on May 5; the accompanying article said, "It was an extra-special occasion, for today is the eighth anniversary of the day that both brothers were liberated from a Nazi concentration camp!"

After two more months of treatments at the Fort MacArthur hospital in San Pedro, Rubin began taking classes at Long Beach City College with his veterans benefits. His leg never returned completely to normal, and he receive a disability payment for the rest of his life. Despite all that he had been through, he was still only twenty-three years old, eager to interact with the opposite sex, see the country, and to just generally enjoy himself.

Rubin worked in his brother's Long Beach liquor store, but his primary objective after being released from the hospital was to become an American citizen. He completed his application for naturalization on November 19, 1953. On the application he reported his address as 4466 Cerritos Drive in Long Beach. His personal description showed that he had gained back much of the weight he had lost in the POW camp. He listed his weight as 158 pounds and his height as five feet six inches.

Rubin's application was approved on November 27. The concentration camp and prisoner of war survivor said, "I always wanted to become a citizen of the United States and when I became a citizen it was one of the happiest days in my life. I think about the United States and I am a lucky person to live here. When I came to America, it was the first time I was free. It was one of the reasons I joined the U. S. Army because I wanted to show my appreciation."

After receiving citizenship, Rubin again came to the attention of the media, who told his story of being a POW and a concentration camp survivor. There was even some talk about making a movie of his life, but time passed and he became forgotten by the public. Rubin by nature was modest and not boastful. He was happy to merely be left alone to continue work at his brother's store, to enjoy the nightlife of Los Angeles, and to travel internationally to see the world as much as possible.

Rubin met Yvonne Meijers at a dance for Jewish singles in early 1962. She too was a Holocaust survivor. Born in Holland, she was hidden by Christian nuns when the Nazis began rounding up Jews. Her parents survived by hiding in the countryside, reclaimed their daughter after the war, and immigrated to the United States in 1957. Rubin and Yvonne married on January 27, 1963, and moved to Garden Grove, California. Over the next three years, they had a son and a daughter. In their spare time, they visited wounded soldiers from the Vietnam War in the Long Beach VA hospital.

In 1981, Rubin attended a reunion of former POWs in Las Vegas. One of the first people he saw was Randal Briere, one of his sergeants in Korea. Neither was aware that the other had survived the war. When Briere found out that Rubin had received two Purple Hearts but not the promised Medal of Honor and Silver Star, he began a campaign to right a more than thirty-year wrong.

Briere contacted fellow ex-POW Leo Cormier, and the two began a search for witnesses of Rubin's valor. They also contacted their congressmen and put together a recommendation for the Medal of Honor for Rubin. In 1985 the Jewish War Veterans of the United States of America joined the effort.

Submissions to the US Army over the years were turned down on the basis of a statute of limitations on Korean War decorations. Several attempts to amend the statutory language were made, but it was not until 1996 that the law was amended to consider decoration claims from earlier wars.

At the same time Rubin's friends were seeking his Medal of Honor, other individuals and groups were lobbying for a review of possible discrimination toward African Americans, Hispanic Americans, Asian Americans, and Jews in the awarding of medals in World War II, Korea, and Vietnam. Finally, Section 552 of the 2002 National Defense Authorization Act required the military to review the records of minority service members who had received the Distinguished Service Cross for possible upgrade to the Medal of Honor.

Although it would be twelve years before the entire review was completed, and the fact that Rubin had not received the DSC, his paperwork was expedited under provisions of the legislation. On September 23, 2005, President Bush presented the Medal of Honor to Rubin in the East Room of the White House. In attendance were Rubin's family, the vice president, military officials, members of Congress, the Hungarian ambassador, and many of the individuals who had long labored to see the medal presented. The president concluded his remarks, saying, "In the years since Abraham Lincoln signed into law the bill establishing the Medal of Honor, we have had many eloquent tributes to what this medal represents. I like Ted's description. He calls it 'the highest honor of the best country in the world.' And today, a grateful America bestows this award on a true son of liberty."

Rubin returned to his home in Garden Grove after the ceremony. He died there at age eighty-six on December 5, 2015, and is buried in Mount Sinai Memorial Park in Los Angeles. On December 16, 2017, the veterans hospital in Long Beach, where he was treated and where he later visited patients, was renamed the Tibor Rubin Veterans Administration Medical Center.

★★★

15

Leonard Martin Kravitz,
Korea, US Army

Company M, 3rd Battalion, 5th Regimental Combat Team, 24th Infantry
  Division
Yangpyong, Korea, March 6–7, 1951
Date Presented: March 18, 2014

CITATION:
*Private First Class Leonard M. Kravitz distinguished himself by acts of gallantry
and intrepidity above and beyond the call of duty while serving as an assistant
machine gunner with Company M, 5th Infantry Regiment, 24th Infantry Division during combat operations against an armed enemy in Yangpyong, Korea on
March 6 and 7, 1951. After friendly elements had repulsed two probing attacks, the
enemy launched a fanatical banzai charge with heavy supporting fire and, despite
staggering losses, pressed the assault with ruthless determination. When the machine gunner was wounded in the initial phase of the action, Private First Class
Kravitz immediately seized the weapon and poured devastating fire into the ranks
of the onrushing assailants. The enemy effected and exploited a breach on the left
flank, rendering the friendly positions untenable. Upon order to withdraw, Private
First Class Kravitz voluntarily remained to provide protective fire for the retiring
elements. Detecting enemy troops moving toward friendly positions, Private First
Class Kravitz swept the hostile soldiers with deadly, accurate fire, killing the entire
group. His destructive retaliation caused the enemy to concentrate vicious fire on
his position and enabled the friendly elements to withdraw. Later, after friendly
troops had returned, Private First Class Kravitz was found dead behind the gun
he had so heroically manned, surrounded by numerous enemy dead. Private First*

Class Kravitz's extraordinary heroism and selflessness at the cost of his own life, above and beyond the call of duty, are in keeping with the highest traditions of military service and reflect great credit upon himself, his unit and the United States Army.

FRIENDS OF LEONARD KRAVITZ worked for sixty years to have his Distinguished Service Cross upgraded to the Medal of Honor. Their efforts not only succeeded for Kravitz but also opened the way for the review of all DSCs awarded to minority service members during World War II, the Korean War, and the Vietnam War.

Born on August 8, 1931, in Brooklyn, New York, the future hero was the son of Joseph and Jean Kaufman Kravitz, who were the children of Ukrainian Jews who had immigrated to the United States. His older brother, Seymour, a World War II veteran, worked as a television news producer for NBC. Seymour's son and Leonard's namesake, Lenny Kravitz, is an award-winning singer, songwriter, actor, and record producer.

Leonard grew up and went to school in the largely Jewish Crown Heights neighborhood of Brooklyn. Rae's Candy Store at the corner of Franklin Avenue and President Street served as the center of the universe for Kravitz and his best friend, Mitchel Libman. In addition to sweets, the candy store front window acted as a community bulletin board for news and announcements.

Kravitz enlisted in the US Army on May 11, 1949. Upon completion of his basic training, he joined the 5th Regimental Combat Team, a regular infantry regiment augmented with tank, artillery, engineer, signal, air defense, quartermaster, military police, medical, and other support units that enabled it to be a self-supporting unit in the field. The 5th RCT deployed to Korea from Hawaii on July 25, 1950, and was initially attached to the 25th Infantry Division. A month later it transferred to the 1st Cavalry Division and in September joined the 24th Infantry Division.

On March 6, 1951, Kravitz's unit occupied defensive positions at Yangpyong when they were attacked by a far larger force that came at them in human waves. Kravitz voluntarily manned a machine gun to cover this company's withdrawal. His last words to his fellow soldiers were, "Get the hell out of here while you can!" For hours the retreating Americans could hear Kravitz's machine gun firing amid the screams of the wounded and dying enemy along with the explosions of grenades and mortar shells they fired at him. When they counterattacked the next morning, his friends found Kravitz dead, still behind his machine gun. He had only six bullets remaining. To his front and flanks were piles of dead enemy soldiers; in his foxhole with him were two more.

Kravitz posthumously received the Distinguished Service Cross. He is buried in Mount Carmel Cemetery (Section 5, Block E, Lot 535, Grave 3) in Queens, New York.

Mitchel Libman, Kravitz's childhood friend, also enlisted in the army and served in Korea. He safely returned to Brooklyn after the war and read about Kravitz's DSC in a post on Rae's Candy Store window. Libman immediately noticed that his friend's valor as detailed in the citation was equal to or surmounted those of many recipients of the Medal of Honor. He and his wife, Marilyn, began a letter-writing campaign to get what he thought Kravitz deserved. The army and Department of Defense answered his letters, reaffirming that Kravitz had received the proper award and that they would take no further action.

Libman became even more determined when his research revealed that, during World War II, Korea, and Vietnam, the army had awarded 138 DSCs to Jews but only 2 Medals of Honor (at the time). He renewed his letter writing and, after he moved to Florida in the 1990s, he sought the assistance of that state's Democratic congressman, Robert Wexler. Congressman Wexler noted that of the 136 Medals of Honor awarded for bravery in Korea, none had gone to a Jewish American. In 2001, Wexler drafted the Leonard Kravitz War Veterans Act, which had the objective of mandating a Pentagon review of DSCs awarded to Jews. The bill never passed, but it did directly influence the adoption of Section 552 of the 2002 National Defense Authorization Act, an order that required the military to review the records of minority service members who had received the Distinguished Service Cross for possible upgrading to the Medal of Honor.

Pentagon officials reviewed Kravitz's DSC along with more than 600 others under the legislation. As a result, on March 18, 2014, Pres. Barack Obama presented the Medal of Honor to Kravitz as one of twenty-three recipients honored that day. Kravitz's niece, Laurie J. Wegner, accepted it on his behalf. In his remarks the president paid a special recognition to Mitchel and Marilyn for their "years writing letters and working with Congress and our military to get this done."

The president also said, "The presentation of our nation's highest military decoration—the Medal of Honor—is always a special occasion. But today, it is truly historic. This is the single largest group of service members to be awarded the Medal of Honor since the Second World War. And with several of these soldiers recognized for their valor during that war, this ceremony is 70 years in the making. As one family member has said, this is long overdue."

President Obama added, "This ceremony reminds us of one of the enduring qualities that makes America great—that makes us exceptional. No nation is perfect, but here in America we confront our imperfections and face a sometimes painful past—including the truth that some of these soldiers fought, and died, for a country that did not always see them as equal. So with each generation we keep on striving to live up to our ideals of freedom and equality, and to recognize the dignity and patriotism of every person, no matter who they are, what they look like, or how they pray."

★★★

16

Jack Howard Jacobs,
Vietnam, US Army

2nd Battalion, 16th Infantry, 9th Infantry Division, Army of the Republic of
  Vietnam

Kien Phong Province, Republic of Vietnam, March 9, 1968

Date Presented: October 9, 1969

CITATION:

*For conspicuous gallantry and intrepidity in action at the risk of his life above and
beyond the call of duty. Capt. Jacobs (then 1st Lt.), Infantry, distinguished himself
while serving as assistant battalion advisor, 2d Battalion, 16th Infantry, 9th Infantry Division, Army of the Republic of Vietnam. The 2d Battalion was advancing
to contact when it came under intense heavy machine gun and mortar fire from
a Viet Cong battalion positioned in well fortified bunkers. As the 2d Battalion
deployed into attack formation its advance was halted by devastating fire. Capt.
Jacobs, with the command element of the lead company, called for and directed air
strikes on the enemy positions to facilitate a renewed attack. Due to the intensity
of the enemy fire and heavy casualties to the command group, including the company commander, the attack stopped and the friendly troops became disorganized.
Although wounded by mortar fragments, Capt. Jacobs assumed command of the
allied company, ordered a withdrawal from the exposed position and established
a defensive perimeter. Despite profuse bleeding from head wounds which impaired
his vision, Capt. Jacobs, with complete disregard for his safety, returned under
intense fire to evacuate a seriously wounded advisor to the safety of a wooded area
where he administered lifesaving first aid. He then returned through heavy automatic weapons fire to evacuate the wounded company commander. Capt. Jacobs*

made repeated trips across the fire-swept open rice paddies evacuating wounded and their weapons. On 3 separate occasions, Capt. Jacobs contacted and drove off Viet Cong squads who were searching for allied wounded and weapons, single-handedly killing 3 and wounding several others. His gallant actions and extraordinary heroism saved the lives of 1 U. S. advisor and 13 allied soldiers. Through his effort the allied company was restored to an effective fighting unit and prevented defeat of the friendly forces by a strong and determined enemy. Capt. Jacobs, by his gallantry and bravery in action in the highest traditions of the military service, has reflected great credit upon himself, his unit, and the U. S. Army.

JACK JACOBS is the only Jewish officer and US Army soldier who is a recipient of the Medal of Honor for actions during the Vietnam War. Born on August 2, 1945, at Crown Heights Hospital in Brooklyn, New York, he spent his early years in a Queens neighborhood dominated by Greek Jews and Catholics. His father, David, a World War II veteran, worked as an engineer by trade. The grandparents of both David and his wife, Marsha, had immigrated to the United States to flee the Eastern European pogroms of the early twentieth century.

Jacobs later wrote that his Yiddish-speaking parents were a mixed marriage—he a Greek Romaniote Jew and she an Ashkenazi Jew. His father never made a great deal of money, and during Jack's early years the family lived in subsidized public housing. According to Jack's autobiography, *If Not Now, When,* he recalled, "I was reared by a mother and father whose parenting objectives were simple and unambiguous: develop seriousness of purpose and a strong sense of responsibility."

In his autobiography, Jacobs nevertheless provides a self-description of being "irreverent, cavalier, and sarcastic." He could have also added "self-deprecating."

In Brooklyn, Jacobs had friends from all kinds of religious and socioeconomic backgrounds. Bored by PS 83, he said of himself, "It was unfortunate, though, that I was at best a difficult, recalcitrant, and recidivist inmate of the prison of childhood."

The Jacobs family moved to Woodbridge, New Jersey, when Jack started the sixth grade. In 1958 he entered Woodbridge High School, where he participated in track and boxing before graduating near the top of his class. Having already reached his adult height of slightly less than five feet six inches, he was not really suited for basketball or football. Upon graduation, Jacobs enrolled in Rutgers University in New Brunswick, New Jersey. He began studying chemical engineering but soon changed his major to political science. During his first year at Rutgers and at the age of only eighteen, Jacobs married Karen Markulin, and over the next five years they would have two children: a boy, David, and a girl, Heather.

In order to support his family and continue as a student, Jacobs held several part-time jobs, including working as a broiler chef, a salesman, and a butcher in a slaughterhouse. He also joined the Reserve Officers' Training Corps. His decision to become a member of the ROTC was based on two primary considerations: First, it paid a small stipend per month in a cadet's final two years. Second, Jacobs felt he had an obligation to his country as a citizen. He also believed that military service was something of a Jewish commandment, a belief that it was deeply ingrained in Judaism and his family.

In his final year in ROTC at Rutgers, Jacobs had to select a specialty branch. He chose infantry because he thought that it was the essence of the army. He also chose a regular army commission over one in the reserves, as it allowed him to go immediately on active duty and to begin receiving a steady army paycheck. Jacobs graduated and was commissioned on June 6, 1966, and reported to Fort Bragg, North Carolina, to join the 82nd Airborne Division as an infantry platoon leader. On a temporary duty assignment, he completed airborne training and the Infantry Basic Officers Course at Fort Benning, Georgia, during the summer of 1966. He discovered in his training that he could run and keep up with the best but that his marksmanship was woefully inferior.

Back with the 82nd, he graduated from jumpmaster school and spent time learning from his company's noncommissioned officers, all of whom had served in Vietnam and some of whom were also veterans of Korea and World War II. In the spring of 1967, Jacobs received orders to attend the US Army Special Warfare School at Fort Bragg and the Defense Language Institute at Fort Bliss, Texas, in preparation for joining the United States Military Assistance Command in Vietnam as an advisor to the Army of South Vietnam.

Jacobs, while not pleased with orders to be an advisor, also regretted the loss of jump pay he had received in the 82nd. Nevertheless, he arrived in Vietnam on September 6, 1967, where he joined the 2nd Battalion, 16th Regiment, of the 9th Vietnamese Infantry Division, a unit posted in the Mekong Delta on the southern tip of South Vietnam. During an early battle between his battalion and a Viet Cong unit, he came face to face with an enemy soldier.

Jacobs drew his .45-caliber pistol and fired the entire magazine. None of the rounds found their target. A soldier next to him killed the soldier with an M-60 machine-gun burst. Jacobs never again carried a pistol; he thereafter favored rifles that fired on automatic. If he could not hit his target with aimed shots, he thought that he might be successful with full volume.

By 1968, Jacobs had survived to be a veteran. All of his experience came to bear on March 9 when he accompanied his battalion's lead company in a search mission. Ambushed by a Viet Cong battalion using small arms, machine guns, and mortars, Jacobs coordinated air and artillery support before he was wounded in the face and head by mortar shrapnel. Despite his wounds—so severe that the blood from his forehead limited his vision— Jacobs dashed forward to rescue a wounded fellow American advisor. He repeated his effort thirteen more times as he pulled Vietnamese officers and enlisted men to safety. Later Jacobs readily admitted being scared during the battle and discounted anyone who claims not to know fear. When asked why he had risked his life to save others, Jacobs quoted first-century Jewish philosopher Rabbi Hillel the Elder. When a man asked what he should do when people keep asking for favors or money, Hillel replied, "If I am not for myself, who will be for me? And if I am only for myself, then what am I? And if not now, when?"

In the midst of the firefight, Jacobs recalled being scared but at the same time remembered Hillel as he thought, "Jacobs, if not for you, then who? And if not now, then when?"

After a series of treatments and hospitalizations, Jacobs reported to Fort Benning, Georgia, where he took command of a company of infantry officer candidates. On October 9, 1969, Pres. Richard Nixon presented the Medal of Honor to Jacobs in a ceremony on the South Lawn of the White House. Jacobs wrote in his biography, "It wasn't until the ceremony had ended that it occurred to me that I was now a very different person. No longer just a soldier, I was now a representative of the 3,400 recipients who'd come before me, of the 450 recipients still surviving at the time, and, most important, of all the soldiers who died defending the nation, From that day on, how I comported myself would have to be wholly a function of being entrusted with a responsibility that I hadn't had the day before."

Jacobs remained at Fort Benning to attend the Infantry Officers Advanced Course, which teaches company-level tactics and staff procedures. He had originally planned to leave the army for law school but put that idea aside, saying, "In those increasingly infrequent times I contemplated leaving the army, I quickly rejected doing it. I loved the mission and I loved the people, and neither the danger nor the insecurity nor even the prospect of having to serve on a mind-numbing staff was sufficient to deter me from staying."

From Fort Benning, Jacobs went back to Rutgers on an army-funded program to earn a master's degree in political science. The army scheduled him for a utilization tour for his education as an instructor at the US Military Academy at West Point, but the position would not be open for another year. Jacob's assignment officer wanted to send him to Korea for a short tour, but he lobbied to be sent back to Vietnam. The army was reluctant to have Medal of Honor recipients return to the war zone, but Jacobs prevailed.

Jacobs arrived in Saigon on July 4, 1972. Once again he avoided duty in the rear and talked his way into becoming the senior advisor of the 1st Battalion of the elite Vietnamese Airborne Division. Jacobs remained with the battalion until the last US personnel, including advisors, were withdrawn from the country in January 1973. By the time he left Vietnam for the final time, Jacobs had become one the most decorated soldiers of the war. In addition to the Medal of Honor, he had earned two Silver Stars, a Bronze Star with "V" device with two oak leaf clusters, an Air Medal, two Purple Hearts, the Army Commendation Medal, and the Combat Infantryman Badge.

Back in the States, Jacobs went straight to the West Point position that had opened earlier than expected. Upon reporting to the academy, where he taught comparative politics and international relations, Jacobs remained on the faculty for three and a half years before being promoted to major and being selected to attend the Command and General Staff College at Fort Leavenworth, Kansas. Although the army had been good to and for Jacobs, the same could not be said for his wife. Karen not only divorced Jacobs but also gave him full custody of their two children. She then disappeared and did not reappear into her children's lives until they were adults.

Jacobs completed CGSC while taking care of his children as a single parent and then received orders to report for duty at the Pentagon. He called his assignment officer and told him that he simply was not going. Jacobs later wrote, "I have been told that when I was three years old, holding my breath and turning blue made no impression on my parents, but at the age of thirty-one, acting like a three-year-old seemed to work remarkably well." The army changed his orders for him to report to the 7th Infantry Division at Fort Ord, California, his being a Medal of Honor perhaps having influence on the assignment decision.

At Fort Ord, Jacobs served as the executive officer of the 2nd Battalion, 32nd Infantry Regiment. Near the end of his tour, he met British exchange officer Capt. Sue Forbes, and they married after she retired from the service. The couple later had a son.

From Fort Ord, Jacobs, now a lieutenant colonel, took command of the 4th Battalion, 10th Infantry Regiment, in Panama in the summer of 1982. He returned to the United States and, after what he called "an interesting one-year assignment in the intelligence business," attended the National War College at Fort McNair in Washington, DC. Upon graduating, Jacobs joined the college's staff as an instructor with the rank of full colonel.

In 1986, Jacobs decided that, while he still loved the army, it was time to look into making more income for his family. He retired on February 1, 1987, and went to work in banking and financial management, including hedge funds. Jacobs also sat on the boards of several for-profit and nonprofit organizations as well as appearing on MSNBC as a military analyst. In May 2012, Jacobs and cowriter David Fisher published *Basic: Surviving Boot Camp and Basic Training*, a history of the US military's basic training programs told primarily through oral histories from army, navy, marine, and air force veterans.

The Beth Sholom Congregation School in Woodbridge, New Jersey, where Jacobs was bar mitzvahed, was renamed the Captain Jack H. Jacobs Hebrew School in November 1969. The dedication plaque reads, "Dedicated in honor of one of our first graduates whose outstanding leadership and distinguished valor while a member of the army brought honor and dignity to American and the Jewish people." In 1997 his hometown dedicated the Township of Woodbridge Jack Jacobs Administration Building.

Jacobs and his wife make their home in New Jersey as of this writing. He still often speaks at schools, civic events, and conferences. In his book he wrote, "To be honest, school principals and business executives find that the attractiveness of an address by Jack Jacobs is not Jack Jacobs at all, but instead my decoration. This is not a bad thing, however. Recipients of the Medal of Honor feel strongly that the award is less a recognition of individual effort than it is representative of the sacrifice and patriotism of all those who have served, many of whom did not survive to talk about it. And as time marches inexorably on, and as the number of living recipients of the award gets smaller, the mission of the remaining recipients—to educate the nation and particularly our youth about service to our republic—becomes more critical."

★★★

17

John Lee Levitow,
Vietnam, US Air Force

3rd Special Operations Squadron, US Air Force
Above Long Binh Army Post, Republic of South Vietnam, February 24, 1969
Date Presented: May 14, 1970

CITATION:

For conspicuous gallantry and intrepidity in action at the risk of his life above and beyond the call of duty. Sgt. Levitow (then A1c.), U. S. Air Force, distinguished himself by exceptional heroism while assigned as a loadmaster aboard an AC-47 aircraft flying a night mission in support of Long Binh Army post. Sgt. Levitow's aircraft was struck by a hostile mortar round. The resulting explosion ripped a hole two feet in diameter through the wing and fragments made over 3,500 holes in the fuselage. All occupants of the cargo compartment were wounded and helplessly slammed against the floor and fuselage. The explosion tore an activated flare from the grasp of a crewmember who had been launching flares to provide illumination for Army ground troops engaged in combat. Sgt. Levitow, though stunned by the concussion of the blast and suffering from over 40 fragment wounds in the back and legs, staggered to his feet and turned to assist the man nearest to him who had been knocked down and was bleeding heavily. As he was moving his wounded comrade forward and away from the opened cargo compartment door, he saw the smoking flare ahead of him in the aisle. Realizing the danger involved and completely disregarding his own wounds, Sgt. Levitow started toward the burning flare. The aircraft was partially out of control and the flare was rolling wildly from side to side. Sgt. Levitow struggled forward despite the loss of blood from his many

★★★

113

*wounds and the partial loss of feeling in his right leg. Unable to grasp the rolling
flare with his hands, he threw himself bodily upon the burning flare. Hugging the
deadly device to his body, he dragged himself back to the rear of the aircraft and
hurled the flare through the open cargo door. At that instant the flare separated
and ignited in the air, but clear of the aircraft. Sgt. Levitow, by his selfless and heroic actions, saved the aircraft and its entire crew from certain death and destruction. Sgt. Levitow's gallantry, his profound concern for his fellowmen, at the risk of
his life above and beyond the call of duty are in keeping with the highest traditions
of the U. S. Air Force and reflect great credit upon himself and the Armed Forces of
his country.*

JOHN LEVITOW is the only US Air Force enlisted man, and one of two Jewish Americans, who earned the Medal of Honor in the Vietnam War. Born on
November 1, 1945, in Hartford, Connecticut, to Lee T. and Marion Levitow,
John graduated from Glastonbury High School in 1965. Family and friends
remember him as reserved, quiet, and unassuming. He initially intended to
join the navy but, after visits with recruiters, changed his mind and on June 6,
1966, enlisted in the U. Air Force at New Haven, Connecticut.

After basic training at Lackland Air Force Base in Texas, Levitow reported
to McGuire Air Force Base, New Jersey, where he trained as a power line
specialist with the 438th Civil Engineering Squadron. On a temporary duty
assignment at Sheppard Air Force Base in Texas, he trained as an aircraft
loadmaster. Levitow then returned to McGuire and joined the 45th Military
Airlift Squadron. While with the 45th, he also trained in aerial delivery and
the loading of nuclear weapons.

In July of 1968, Levitow reported to the 3rd Special Operations Squadron
at Bien Hoa Air Base in the Republic of Vietnam as a loadmaster. The 3rd
Squadron flew the AC-47, the military version of the DC-3, which had been
in the inventory since World War II. These aircraft, call sign Spooky, originally designed as transports, were modified to become flying attack platforms.
Three 7.62-mm General Electric miniguns were mounted so as to fire through
two rear window openings and the side cargo door, on the pilot's (left) side of
the aircraft, to provide close air support for ground troops. The pilot fired the
guns, either singly or together, with a control on his yoke in the cockpit while
a copilot, navigator, and flight engineer assisted as needed. A loadmaster and
two gunners were stationed in the rear of the aircraft to assist in gun failures
or other problems and to deploy illumination flares.

Each of Spooky's three miniguns could be selectively fired at a rate of either 50 or 100 rounds per second. Cruising in an overhead left-hand orbit at an air speed of 120 knots and at an altitude of 3,000 feet, the C-47 gunship could put a bullet into every square yard of a football field-sized target in less than ten seconds. With every fifth round a tracer, the arc of bullets from the gunship to the ground, appeared to be a continuous red stream, thus originating the term "hosing down the target." Spooky's basic load of 24,000 rounds allowed it to loiter over a target area, firing intermittently, for hours.

Along with the miniguns, each Spooky carried up to forty-five MK-24 magnesium flares that measured three feet long, weighed twenty-seven pounds, and burned at 4,000 degrees to produce a light of two million candlepower for up to three minutes. The delivery system for the MK-24s was simple—the loadmaster armed the flare and dropped the flare out the cargo door when the pilot signaled by flashing a cargo compartment light.

On February 24, 1969, Levitow filled in for the regular loadmaster aboard Spooky 71, flying a night mission over Ton Son Nhut Air Base. When notified that the nearby American installation at Long Binh was under mortar attack, Spooky 71 changed its course and began orbiting over the base. On the command of the pilot, Maj. Kenneth Carpenter, Levitow and the gunners began arming MK-24 flares and tossing them out the cargo door. Levitow set the timer of a flare and handed it to Amn. Ellis C. Owen, who held it with his finger extended through the pull ring attached to the safety pin.

Suddenly, an 82-mm mortar round exploded into the aircraft's right wing, sending shrapnel into the fuselage and wounding Levitow and the two gunners. The explosion jarred the MK-24 from Ellis's hands, pulling the safety pin and arming the canister. Levitow realized that the armed canister rolling around the fuselage would detonate within seconds and its heat would cook off the nearly 20,000 remaining rounds of ammunition as well as burning a hole through the rear deck to the aircraft control cables below. Despite suffering from more than forty shrapnel wounds in his right thigh and leg and almost blinded by smoke from both the explosion and from the burning MK-24 fuse, Levitow crawled to the canister, hugged it to his body, and dragged himself to the rear cargo door. He thrust the canister into the night, away from the plane, just before it ignited. Major Carpenter managed to land the aircraft safely with its more than 3,500 shrapnel holes and a three-foot hole in the wing. He would later say, "I had the aircraft in a 30-degree bank, and how Levitow managed to get to the flare and throw it out, I'll never know."

Levitow spent sixteen weeks in a US Air Force hospital in Tachikawa, Japan. When he recovered, he returned to Vietnam and flew several more missions before being grounded when his commander learned he was being considered for the Medal of Honor. When Levitow completed his tour in July 1969, he was a veteran of more than 180 Spooky sorties. Back in the States, he joined the 14th Military Airlift Wing at Norton Air Force Base, California, as a loadmaster aboard C-141s before his discharge in April 1970.

The US Air Force emphasizes training as a prerequisite for promotion, and Levitow's graduation from loadmaster school had been left out of his records by error. Thus, he served as an airman 1st class for his entire year in Vietnam and for nearly all of his final two years in uniform. He was not promoted to sergeant until two weeks before his discharge.

Shortly after leaving the air force, Levitow joined eleven other service members on May 14, 1970, Armed Forces Day, in the East Room of the White House for the presentation of their Medals of Honor. Pres. Richard Nixon said, "Today we honor the brave men, the men who, far beyond the call of duty, served their country magnificently in a war very far away, in a war which is one, many times, not understood and not supported by some in this country. I believe also as I stand here, that as time goes on, millions more of your countrymen will look back at the experience that you have participated in and they will reach the conclusion that you served the cause of the land of the free by being brave, brave far beyond the call of duty; so brave that you received the very highest award that this Nation can provide."

Levitow returned to Glastonbury, Connecticut, after the ceremony to a parade and hero's welcome. Over the next three decades he and his wife, Barbara, had two children as he worked tirelessly for state and federal veterans agencies and became the legislative liaison and director of planning for the Connecticut Department of Veterans Affairs.

Today those airmen who finish in the top one percent of the Air Force Enlisted Professional Military Education programs, including Airman Leadership School, the NCO Academy, and the Senior NCO Academy, are eligible for the John Levitow Award. The 737th Training Group Headquarters building at Lackland Air Force Base, Texas, is named in his honor, and he is included in the Hurlburt Field Walk of Fame in Florida and the Scott Air Force Base Airlift/Tanker Hall of Fame in Illinois. He is also remembered in his hometown. The former Hartford-Laurel Post 45 of the Jewish War Veterans of the United States of American has been renamed John Levitow Post 45. A bridge on West Street in Rocky Hill, Connecticut, bears his name, and the City of Glastonbury erected a monument to him on the town green. Levitow was invited to and attended every US presidential inauguration for the rest of his life.

On January 23, 1998, in a ceremony at the Boeing Facility in Long Beach, California, the air force named a C-17 Globemaster III *The Spirit of Sgt. John L. Levitow*. This was the first time an airplane had been named in honor of an enlisted man. In his remarks Gen. Walter Kross, the commander of the Air Mobility Command, said,

> We can easily call Sgt. John Levitow a hero, but he has continuously requested that he doesn't want to be known as a hero. His life amounts to much more than those 10 heroic minutes. So, I'll honor his request and tell you some of the other reasons why his name ought to be on this aircraft. He was a young airman simply doing his duty, flying a mission in the middle of the night in some far off land. Each night, he didn't get to sleep in his own bed back home or have a hot meal with his family. Every day, he spent working hard, getting dirty and getting tired in the service of his country.

Kross concluding saying that Levitow risked his life for "the soldiers on the ground in countless other missions—people he never met." He added, "His life has been one of tireless volunteerism—a role model, a mentor—with other enlisted professional education at the center of everything he did."

Levitow emotionally responded, "I'm a firm believer that I do represent the enlisted corps. I'm just lucky. Luck is all it is. It's very easy to do something and not be recognized. I'm sure there are many people who have served, have done things that have been simply amazing and never been recognized. Lucky was that I had somebody that recognized it and put me in for it."

On November 8, 2000, Levitow, after a year and a half of fighting cancer, died at age fifty-five at the Connecticut State Veterans Home in Rocky Hill. His is buried in Arlington National Cemetery (Section 66, Site 7107) in Washington, DC.

As a eulogy for Levitow, chief master sergeant of the US Air Force, Jim Finch, said, "John Levitow for years has been woven into the fabric of enlisted heritage. Through his heroic efforts, he was the embodiment our core value 'service before self.' His name has become synonymous with excellence, and his legacy will continue to live in the hearts and minds of all Air Force members today and well into the future."

Sec. of the Air Force Whit Peters added, "Sergeant Levitow served during a war in which heroic tasks were commonplace, but by any standard, his courage that night was extraordinary. His selfless actions saved not only his life but the lives of seven others. For decades he has been an inspiration to all our airmen—enlisted, officers, and civilians."

Although Levitow was proud of his Jewish heritage and readily claimed to be a Jew, he did not follow the tenants and traditions of Judaism. He raised his children as Catholics, and his headstone at Arlington is engraved with the Christian cross rather than the Star of David.

On May 22, 2008, Connecticut governor M. Jodi Rell dedicated a new veterans health care center in Rocky Hill named in Levitow's honor. Governor Rell said, "John Levitow is a true Connecticut hero and treasure. It is the totality of his life—most especially his loyal and tireless service to Connecticut veterans after he left the military—that make this tribute so fitting. Despite his enormous courage, he was a very unassuming, humble public servant who always put others first."

Dr. Linda S. Schwartz, commissioner of the Connecticut Department of Veterans Affairs, added, "This quiet, generous hero contributed much to the lives of veterans in our state and nation. He served for years as a model and mentor to thousands in the enlisted ranks of the United States Air Force. His deeds and actions on that night long ago continue to inspire and enrich our nation."

PART 2

Medal of Honor Recipients, Likely Jewish but Not Confirmed

★★★

18

Isaac Gause,
Civil War, US Army

Company E, 2nd Ohio Volunteer Cavalry Regiment
Near Berryville, Virginia, September 13, 1864
Date Presented: September 19, 1864

CITATION:
Capture of the colors of the 8th South Carolina Infantry while engaged in a reconnaissance along the Berryville and Winchester Pike.

ISAAC GAUSE enlisted in the Union army a few months after the first shots were fired in the Civil War and served in nearly every theater of the conflict until five months after it concluded. Born on December 9, 1843, in Trumbull County, Ohio, he moved with his parents to Mahoning County at the age of seven and then to Goshen Township to live with his Uncle Elijah at age fourteen. Little else is known about his pre-military experience. Later census reports state that Gause's father was born in either Germany or Ohio and his mother in Ohio. His military records show that he stood five feet eight inches tall, had gray eyes, and could read and write. Apparently he picked up some carpentry skills as a youth, as that is what is listed as his occupation in all of his military documents and census records.

On August 10, 1861, four months before his eighteenth birthday, Gause enlisted as a private in Company E, 2nd Ohio Volunteer Cavalry Regiment at Camp Wade near Cleveland. For the next four years, Gause and the 2nd Ohio fought in every region and in many of the primary battles of the war. From Ohio to Kentucky, to Missouri, to Kansas, to Indian Territory, to Tennessee, and to Virginia, the 2nd Ohio performed its duties of reconnaissance, defensive delaying actions, pursuit of defeated enemy forces, offensive actions, and long-distance raiding against rebel lines of communications, railroads, and supply depots. In addition to participating in the major battles—Wilderness, Spotsylvania Court House, Shenandoah Valley, and Cedar Creek—the 2nd Ohio engaged William Quantrill's guerillas at Independence, Missouri, fought Confederate Native American commander Stand Waite in Indian Territory, and pursued John Hunt Morgan's cavalry raid through Kentucky, Indiana, and Ohio. In the final days of the war the 2nd Ohio followed the retreat of Robert E. Lee's army from Petersburg and was present at their surrender at Appomattox Court House.

Most of what is known about Gause during this period comes from his military records and his own writings. In 1908, more than forty years after his war experiences, Gause published *Five Years with Five Armies: Army of the Frontier, Army of the Potomac, Army of the Missouri, Army of the Ohio, Army of the Shenandoah*. In the book's preface, Gause explains that he did not keep a diary during the war and that his book is "guided almost entirely by memory" and that its purpose is to show the long campaigns, privations, and engagements during his four years of service.

In his preface he admits that he had a rural background and knew little about the outside world or the military. Gause wrote that he grew up in communities where many of his neighbors were abolitionists. He had friends who had friends or family members who were members of John Brown's raid on Harpers Ferry in 1859. He, however, enlisted with "no ambition but to do my part in coercing the seceded States to return to the Union."

Much of his book is like that of any other soldier's in any other war—the boredom of camp, the poor quality or lack of food and clothing, and the interaction with his fellow soldiers. Gause also pontificates on the abilities of his horses and his affection for them.

Gause completed his first enlistment on December 31, 1863, and reenlisted the next day. In his book he wrote that reenlisting provided a bounty of $400 and a thirty-day home leave. However, his primary reason for reenlisting was a patriotic one: "I had left home to see the Union preserved, and anything short of that was no reward for me."

In Washington, DC, on April 29, 1864, Gause and his fellow cavalrymen received fresh horses and equipment. The next day they were issued Spencer breech-loading rifles, each of which had a magazine containing seven .52-caliber primed metallic cartridges.

On July 4, 1864, Gause received a promotion to corporal. Two months later he earned his Medal of Honor. Although the official citation is only one sentence in length, a more detailed account is included in *Deeds of Valor*, edited by W. F. Beyer and O. F. Keydel. In their book, published in 1901, the editors included this first-person account by Gause:

> On the morning of September 13, 1864, I was sent forward with seven men to reconnoiter the enemy's position on the north side of the creek near Berryville, Virginia. After we had crossed the creek we captured the Confederate outpost, from whom we learned that the troops in camp were the Eighth South Carolina. Sending our prisoners to the rear in charge of two men, I rode rapidly, expecting my five remaining comrades would follow me around the woods which were at the top of the ridge half a mile beyond the creek. Presently I discovered that I was alone, my comrades having left the pike, going to the left around the south side of the woods. I also saw our main force under General McIntosh had followed them and had attacked the enemy, who were on a hill to the west. Just at this time I reached the slope on the east and north of the woods, when I was fired at from a thicket, whereupon I rode into a ravine at the west of the pike and jumped my horse over a ditch to get under cover. As my horse landed on the other side of the ditch he went to his knees and I thought he had been hit; but he came up all right and I followed the ravine until I got back to the pike, where I met General McIntosh and his staff and reported to him that the enemy had a cavalry reserve north of the woods and that they were getting ready to come to the assistance of the troops on the hill and in the woods. "But," I said, "we can get around the woods and intercept them." Accordingly, Company E of my regiment, under command of Major Nettleton, was ordered to the place directed. Our movement was quickly made, and sure enough we reached the northwest corner of the ravine which I had before visited, entering a larger one running north just in time to intercept the Confederates moving north toward their cavalry. The heads of our columns were not more than fifty yards apart. We charged at them and were met by a withering fire, but this did not stagger us, and their line began to break. "Come on boys!" I yelled, and with wild whoops we doubled our speed. Just then the cavalry reserve began to pop at us from the rear, but at this time also our main force came up from the south and west,

and the Confederates between our lines began to flee in every direction. In the mix-up that followed I captured the color-guard and a stand of colors, and this won for me the Medal of Honor.

Sydney G. Gumpertz, a fellow Civil War veteran and Medal of Honor recipient, also included Gause's story in *The Jewish Legion of Valor*, published in 1934. Gumpertz begins his entry on Gause with the official citation and then continues,

> Sergeant Gause was born on December 9, 1843, in Trumbull County, Ohio, and was a corporal of Company E, 2nd Ohio Cavalry. On the morning of the fight he was sent with seven men on a reconnaissance to try and learn the position of the enemy on the north side of the creek. Getting across the stream, the party dashed for and captured the enemy's videttes (mounted sentries), and then galloping ahead he became separated from his men, but fortunately learning the exact position of the enemy he rode through the woods until meeting General McIntosh, he told him what he had discovered. A spirited fight was promptly inaugurated, and soon became a close hand-to-hand struggle. Corporal Gause was in the very front, and in the midst of the melee succeeded in compelling the surrender of the color-bearer of the Carolina regiment and took the flag also.

On September 19, Gause reported to the office of Sec. of War Edwin M. Stanton, who presented him the Medal of Honor. Following a four-day furlough, during which time he received the actual medal after it had been engraved at the Adjutant General's Office, Gause returned to his unit and participated in some of the war's final battles and skirmishes.

On March 29, 1865, the 2nd Ohio was in pursuit of Lee's army in its retreat from Petersburg to Appomattox. The war was only a few days from its conclusion when a musket ball struck Gause's left ankle. He managed to remount his horse and make his way to a field hospital at Dinwiddie Court House, where he joined one of the officers from his regiment who had also been wounded. Gause took his overcoat, with his Medal of Honor in its pocket, and placed it under the officer's head. When Gause was evacuated to Hancock's station, he left the coat and medal behind. He would never see it again. In September 20, 1897, the War Department issued him a replacement Medal of Honor.

Gause received treatment for his leg wound at Glenwood Hospital in Washington, DC, and then at Philadelphia's Chestnut Hill Hospital. He was unable to return to his regiment to march with them in the Grand Review of the

Armies in Washington, DC, on May 23. Gause did rejoin his company for their transfer from Virginia to Missouri at the end of the month. In Missouri, the 2nd Ohio promoted Gause to sergeant. On September 11, 1865, Gause and the 2nd Ohio were mustered out of the service at Benton Barracks, Missouri, and were transported to Columbus, Ohio where they received their final pay and were disbanded.

The army authorized the 2nd Ohio, as a cavalry regiment, a little more than 1,000 officers and enlisted men. According to its official records, 2,504 men served in the regiment at one time or another during the war. When it was mustered out, the 2nd Ohio had a strength of 757. During the war, the regiment lost a total of 267 men—7 officers and 76 enlisted men killed or mortally wounded, 5 officers and 179 enlisted men to disease.

Few records of Gause's activities exist for a quarter century after his discharge. There is evidence, however, that Gause put his experience as a horse soldier to use. His veteran's pension records show that he made his way to Houston, Texas, shortly after his discharge in Ohio. The only account of what he did in the Lone Star State comes from his book, in which he compares his experiences there to the time in 1862 when the 2nd Ohio captured a herd of cattle in Indian Territory and then drove the beefs to Fort Scott, Kansas: "I have been engaged in cow hunting on the frontiers of Texas, made three trips across the plains, and had some lively drives many years afterwards." Participating in these cattle drives, which occurred from 1866 and until the late 1880s, from Texas to the railroads in Kansas did not preclude Gause from continuing to list his occupation as a carpenter.

The 1890 census had Gause living in Hillsborough, located in southwestern New Mexico. On June 13, 1894, the Western Branch of the National Home for Disabled Volunteer Soldiers in Leavenworth, Kansas, admitted Gause "with a gunshot wound to his left leg." It is not clear, but this was likely complications from his Civil War wound rather than a new injury.

On January 6, 1896, the Leavenworth home transferred Gause to the Government Hospital for the Insane in Washington, DC, with no details concerning his mental problems. The 1900 census records Gause as a patient at the hospital on June 9. Hospital records show that he was transferred back to the Western Branch in Leavenworth on August 16. Apparently, he recovered from his mental problems because over the next eight years he wrote and published his Civil War memoir.

The Southern Branch of the National Home for Disabled Volunteer Soldiers at Hampton, Virginia, admitted Gause on June 6, 1913, and transferred him to the Mountain Branch in Johnson City, Tennessee, in 1918, where the 1920 census listed him as a resident. Gause died there on April 23, 1920, of chronic myocarditis—inflammation of the heart muscle. He never married. His final documents at the Mountain Branch home listed Jesse W. Cummings of Washington, DC, as his next of kin. Gause is buried in Arlington National Cemetery (Section 17, Site 19595) in Washington, DC.

There is debate as to whether Gause was a Jew. The Congressional Medal of Honor Society states that Gause's status as a Jew is "unconfirmed," and there is evidence to both support and oppose that status. In his 1895 book, *The American Jew as Patriot, Soldier, and Citizen,* Simon Wolf lists seven Jewish Medal of Honor recipients and states, "I am not prepared to say how many soldiers of the Jewish faith were honored by such medals, but I can mention seven who have come under my notice." Although he misspells Gause as Gans, he does correctly note his regiment and the actions that earned his medal.

Gumpertz, in *The Jewish Legion of Valor,* includes Gause as a Jew in two entries. Seymour Brody, board member of the Jewish War Veterans National Museum of American Jewish Military History and former member of the National Executive Committee of the Jewish War Veterans of the United States of America, includes Gause as a Jew in his 2004 book, *Jewish Heroes & Heroines of America.* It is also noteworthy that Gause's home state of Ohio had a sizable Jewish population in the nineteenth century and that it provided more Jewish men to the Union army than any state other than New York.

Gause's headstone at Arlington is of the generation that did not include religious symbols. Nowhere in his Civil War memoir does the cavalryman mention his religious beliefs. He does write that his mother's brother raised him as a teenager and states that his uncle had been raised a Quaker. It is also worth mentioning that if Gause was a Jew, he was certainly not kosher. In more than a half-dozen instances in his book, he mentions eating and enjoying ham and bacon, often cooked in communal pots. Of course, in time of war, food is often sparse and soldiers, regardless of religion, are forced to consume whatever is available.

None of Gause's official military records, like most of that era, have any listing of religious preference. The records of the US National Homes for Disabled Volunteer Soldiers for the period 1866–1938 have entries for Gause for his original admittance at Leavenworth and his death twenty-five years later in Tennessee. Both documents, under Domestic History, under religion, have "Prot." However, both documents note his age incorrectly as fifty, and the second document appears to be copied from the first.

Considering all the evidence, the Congressional Medal of Honor Society's evaluation of Gause's status as a Jew as "unconfirmed" seems valid. Claims of Wolf and Gumpertz, who likely either knew Gause or some of his comrades, seem to validate the cavalryman's religion. While it does not seem that his mother was Jewish, his father might very well have been.

★★★

19

Henry Heller,
Civil War, US Army

Company A, 66th Ohio Volunteer Infantry Regiment
Chancellorsville, Virginia, May 2, 1863
Date Presented: July 29, 1892

CITATION:
One of a party of four who, under heavy fire, voluntarily brought into the Union lines a wounded Confederate officer from whom was obtained valuable information concerning the position of the enemy.

HENRY HELLER earned his Medal of Honor not by killing the enemy but rather by showing compassion in rescuing a wounded opponent. Little is known of Heller's early life other than he was born on May 14, 1841, to parents William and Catherine Mays Heller in Clarion County, Pennsylvania. The family soon moved to nearby Urbana, Ohio, and apparently Heller grew up on a farm, as later census documents list his occupation as "farmer."

Heller enlisted for a period of three years on October 20, 1861, at Camp McArthur outside of Urbana and, on December 26, 1861, joined Company A, 66th Ohio Volunteer Infantry Regiment. The 66th Ohio, organized at Camp McArthur a week earlier on the 17th, participated in the battles of Bull Run and Antietam in 1862 and at Chancellorsville and Gettysburg in 1863. In August 1863 the regiment helped subdue the draft riots in New York City and in October joined the Chattanooga–Lookout Mountain–Missionary Ridge Campaign in Tennessee. From there they participated in the siege and battle of Atlanta before marching with Gen. William T. Sherman through

Georgia to Savannah. From there, the 66th Ohio maneuvered northward into the Carolinas, being present for the surrender of the army of Gen. Joseph E. Johnston at Durham, North Carolina, on April 26, 1865. On May 24, the regiment marched through Washington, DC, as part of the Grand Review of the Armies.

During the war the 66th Ohio lost a total of 245 men. Five officers and 96 enlisted soldiers were killed or mortally wounded in action while another officer and 143 enlisted men died of disease.

Heller was not with the regiment in its final months. He completed his enlistment on December 17, 1864, and was mustered out of the army near Savannah, Georgia. Dedication and bravery marked his service. He advanced in rank from private to sergeant and on May 2, 1863, performed the actions that earned him and three fellow soldiers the Medal of Honor—although the medals would not be officially issued until after a review on July 29, 1892.

In *Deeds of Valor,* editors W. F. Beyer and O. F. Kendal wrote about the action in a chapter titled "Soldiers as Good Samaritans." They said, "At Chancellorsville, four members of Company A, Sixty-sixth Ohio Volunteer Infantry, Wallace W. Cranston, Henry Heller, Thomas Thompson, and Elisha B. Seaman, accomplished a deed, which won the admiration of their comrades, the gratitude of the enemy, and a Medal of Honor from the Government." The editors state that the story was told by Private Cranston as follows:

At about nine o'clock in the morning, the Twenty-third North Carolina Infantry came up the plank road, and marched by platoons to within about seventy-five yards of our works. A few charges of grape and canister from a Pennsylvania battery stationed with our division on the plank road, served to stop their progress. In their retreat they left a Confederate soldier on the road. The poor fellow's piteous cries for help attracted the attention of the commanding general, who was passing along the lines. He asked for volunteers to go out and bring him in. "The roads are full of rebels," said he, "but if you go boldly down unarmed, they will know that you are after a wounded man and will surely not be so inhuman as to fire on you who are bringing relief to one of their own men." With three of my companions, I volunteered for the service. We laid off our accouterments, and, with two army blankets for stretchers, marched to where the man lay, in plain view of the enemy. We succeeded in bringing him back alive, and took him to the Chancellor House, which was then being used as a field hospital. After we had disposed of our wounded rebel, we rejoined our regiment, and very soon the battle opened in earnest all along the line. It continued for several hours with the greatest fury until we were driven in disorder from the field.

The Medals of Honor citations for the four good Samaritans states that "valuable information concerning the position of the enemy" was obtained from the rescued officer. In Cranston's narrative, he relates, however, that all did not end well, writing, "The Chancellor House took fire from the rebel shells during the engagement, and burned to the ground, and I suppose this poor rebel soldier, with many of our own wounded must have perished in the flames."

Although wounded in the right elbow during the Battle of Chattanooga on November 24–25, Heller recovered sufficiently to return to his unit to complete his enlistment. He mustered out of the service on December 17, 1864. Less than a month later, back in Ohio, he married Mariam Conover on January 14, 1865. They settled near Urbana, where Heller farmed for the remainder of his life. He died on December 14, 1895, and is buried in the Kings Creek Baptist Church Cemetery just north of Urbana.

There is no record of Heller's religion in his military records, and in the same manner as his fellow Medal of Honor recipient Isaac Gause, there is debate as to whether Heller was a Jew. Like Gause, the Congressional Medal of Honor Society states that Heller's status as a Jew is "unconfirmed." Gumpertz, Wolf, and Brody all state that Heller was Jewish. An entry in the 1906 edition of the *Jewish Encyclopedia* titled "Distinguished Jews of Ohio," by Cyrus Adler and H. G. Friedman, lists Heller as a Jew.

Yet Heller is buried in a Protestant cemetery. There is also a review of Brody's *Jewish Heroes and Heroines of America* by a distant cousin of Heller who claims his relative was a descendant of a long line of Reformed Church members who originated in Switzerland.

It is doubtful that any additional information on Heller's religion will surface at this late date.

20

George Geiger,
Indian Wars, US Army

Company H, 7th US Cavalry Regiment
Little Bighorn, Montana, June 25, 1876
Date Presented: October 5, 1878

CITATION:
With three comrades during the entire engagement courageously held a position that secured water for the command.

SGT. GEORGE GEIGER served for four years in the Civil War, including his time being held prisoner in the infamous Confederate Andersonville Prison, and then for ten years in the postwar army before earning the Medal of Honor as a member of George Custer's command at the Battle of the Little Bighorn. Despite his long and distinguished service, little is known of Geiger's early life or of his years after he left the army.

Born in 1843, likely on January 1, although this date is questionable, in Cincinnati, Ohio, Geiger enlisted as a private in Company A, 47th Ohio Volunteer Infantry Regiment on June 15, 1861. Geiger, at age eighteen, must have been anxious to either get out of Cincinnati or join the army because he enlisted in the 47th two months before its formal organization at Camp Dennison, Ohio, on August 13. His enlistment records state that he stood five feet five inches tall, had a dark complexion and gray eyes, and was literate. Upon completion of training, Geiger and the 47th deployed to western Virginia, where they remained until joining the siege and attack on Vicksburg, Mississippi, in the summer of 1863. In January 1864 the regiment marched into eastern Tennessee, where Geiger and others, also completing their three-year enlistments, reenlisted on March 8. They were granted home furloughs from March 18 to May 13.

With its reenlisted veterans and new volunteers, the 47th Ohio took part in the Battle of Atlanta, where Geiger became a prisoner of war on July 22. Transferred to the Camp Sumter prison camp, better known as Andersonville, Geiger survived the harsh conditions that resulted in the deaths of 13,000 of 45,000 prisoners. It is uncertain how long he was there and how he left. Some records indicate that Geiger was held for only a little more than two months before rejoining his regiment. Geiger may have escaped, or he may have been liberated during Sherman's March to the Sea. It is verifiable from his military records, however, that he, along with the rest of the 47th Ohio, was discharged at Little Rock, Arkansas, on August 11, 1865.

Geiger remained a private for the duration of his two enlistments in the Civil War. Details of his service have been lost to the passage of time, but from what information that is available, it is obvious that Geiger was a survivor. In addition to living through a time at Andersonville, Geiger was one of only 120 men of the original 870 who composed the 47th Regiment who still stood in the ranks at war's end. In addition to those who did not reenlist after three years, the regiment lost a total of 219 men—2 officers and 80 enlisted men killed or mortally wounded in action and another officer and 136 men felled by disease.

Nothing is known of Geiger's subsequent activities until he enlisted for three years as a private in Troop M of the 7th US Cavalry Regiment on November 29, 1867, in St. Louis, Missouri. Various documents list Geiger's occupation over his life as a "teamster," so it is likely that this was his line of work before his enlistment in the would-be famous 7th Cavalry, which had been constituted the previous year as a part of the expansion of the Regular Army following the demobilization of Civil War volunteer units. Posted primarily at Fort Riley, Kansas, the 7th Cavalry engaged Native Americans, including the South Cheyenne at the Battle of the Washita in 1868, before moving to the Deep South in 1871 in support of Reconstruction.

Geiger completed his enlistment and was discharged on November 29, 1872, in Unionville, South Carolina. His civilian life was short-lived. Nineteen days later, on December 18, 1872, Geiger reenlisted in Louisville, Kentucky, and reported to Troop H of his former 7th Cavalry Regiment. Both of Geiger's post–Civil War enlistments came in late November. This was typical of many soldiers of the time. With winter coming on and jobs scarce in the cold months, the army provided a job, pay, and a warm place to sleep—at least when not in the field.

The 7th Cavalry moved its headquarters to Fort Abraham Lincoln in Dakota Territory in 1873 from where they participated in the Black Hill Expedition in 1874 and the Sioux Wars of 1876–1877. In the spring of 1876 the army deployed three columns into southeastern Montana to confront hostile Sioux tribe members and to force them back onto their reservations. On June 17, Gen. Alfred Terry dispatched Lt. Col. George Armstrong Custer and his 7th Cavalry Regiment as an advanced reconnaissance.

Custer, who had earned brevet general's stars while in his early twenties in the Civil War by making quick decisions and acting aggressively, had experienced success in previous battles with the Native Americans by quickly attacking before they could retreat and disperse. On June 25 he neared a large encampment of Sioux on the Little Bighorn River. Little did Custer know that he was vastly outnumbered and that the Indians had recently acquired repeating rifles that were superior to the single-shot weapons in his command.

He did not wait for the rest of Terry's column but rather immediately deployed for an attack. Custer divided his command into three elements. Maj. Marcus Reno led one column to the south of the Sioux camp while Custer advanced along the north bank. A smaller unit, including the regiment's pack train and Geiger's H Troop—led by Capt. Frederick Benteen—followed Reno. Reno's column struck the south end of the camp but was quickly repulsed and sent into an unorderly retreat to the bluffs above the river. The soldiers were endangered of being overrun when Benteen arrived to reinforce their small perimeter. Benteen had been ordered by a message from Custer to come to his support but was unable to make it further than Reno's position. Shortly after Reno and Benteen joined forces, they heard a battle raging to their north. It would not be until the 27th, two days later, that they became aware of the fight—what became known as "Custer's Last Stand"—and the deaths of his entire column of more than 200 men.

Reno and Benteen continued to fight for their very survival for the remainder of the 25th and on into the 27th. Sgt. Charles Windolph described the fight and Geiger's valor in *I Fought with Custer*:

"Along about this time our thirty or forty wounded men began crying out again for water. "H" Troop held the hill here on the southwest. There was a draw that ran down the west side of the hill to the river. It was rough and exposed and it looked like a dead cinch that anyone who tried to work his way down that draw to the river would be killed. Indians concealed in bushes across the river were firing up at us, and they had every foot of this draw and the river bank covered. But we had to do something for those men who were wounded and crying for water.

Finally, Captain Benteen called for volunteers. I think there were seventeen of us altogether who stepped forward. He detailed four of us from "H" who were extra good marksmen to take up an exposed position on the brow of the hill, facing the river. We were to stand up and not only draw the fire of the Indians below, but we were to pump as much lead as we could into the bushes where the Indians were hiding, while the water party hurried down to the draw, got their buckets and canteens filled, and then made their way back. It just happened that the four of us who were posted on the hill were all German boys—Geiger, Meckling, Voit, and myself. None of us four were wounded, although we stood exposed on that ridge for more than twenty minutes, and they threw plenty of lead at us. Several of the water party, however, were badly wounded, although we kept a steady fire into the bushes where the Indians were hiding. Each of us was given a Congressional Medal of Honor.

Following the fight on the Little Bighorn, Geiger completed his enlistment and received an honorable discharge at Fort Buford, South Dakota, on December 18, 1877. He settled in Princeton, Indiana, where census records list his occupation as "teamster." By 1889, Geiger had returned to Ohio, where he married Augusta Krick in Cincinnati. There is no record of their having children. His military pension records list his nearest relative as a half-brother, Edward Metzer, of 1208 West 7th Street in Cincinnati.

In 1897, Geiger transferred from the Middle Branch of the National Home for Disabled Volunteer Soldiers in Marion, Indiana, to the Central Branch of home in Dayton, Ohio—also known as the Dayton Soldiers' Home and later the Dayton VA Medical Center. Geiger sought treatment for chronic dysentery and rheumatism attributed to his confinement in Andersonville Prison. He died at the soldiers home on January 23, 1904, and is buried in Dayton National Cemetery (Section N, Row 20, Grave 47). There is no known photograph of the heroic cavalryman.

The Congressional Medal of Honor Society lists Geiger, like fellow Medal of Honor recipients Gause and Heller, as "May have been Jewish; unconfirmed." Seymour Brody, in *Jewish Heroes & Heroines of America*, writes about Geiger, "There is very little known of him except for his bravery as recorded in the records of the military and that he was Jewish." Geni Family Tree genealogy has Geiger listed as Jewish, as does Aish.com. Sydney Gumpertz, in *Jewish Legion of Valor,* covers the Jewish heroes of the Civil War, Spanish-American War, and World War I but makes no comment about the Indian Wars. Circumstantial evidence is that Geiger came from a region of Ohio with a relative high Jewish population.

The only entry about religion on Geiger's military and veterans documents is a *P* under "Religion" in the Domestic History section of the Admissions Register for the Middle Branch of the US National Home for Disabled Volunteer Soldiers from 1900. This may have been a mistake, like those made on many of these types of documents, or perhaps Geiger did not identify himself as a Jew to avoid the bias of the medical and administrative staff. Several people who claim to be distant relatives of Geiger currently live in Nebraska. They note that most of the family today is Catholic but that they have no idea about Geiger's religion.

★

PART 3

Medal of Honor Recipients, Possibly Jewish

★★★

21

Abraham Greenawalt,
Civil War, US Army

Company G, 104th Ohio Volunteer Infantry Regiment

Franklin, Tennessee, November 11, 1864

Date Presented: February 13, 1865

CITATION:
Capture of corps headquarters flag (C.S.A.).

OF ALL THE JEWISH, or possibly Jewish, Medal of Honor recipients, Abraham Greenawalt is the least known and about whom the minimal amount of information is available. There is no known image of Greenawalt as a Civil War soldier. Even the citation for his medal, consisting of six words and an abbreviation, is among the shortest of all the recipients.

Born on February 23, 1834, in Montgomery County, Pennsylvania, Greenawalt enlisted in the service for three years at Salem, Ohio, on August 7, 1862. He then reported to the 104th Ohio Volunteer Infantry Regiment at Camp Massillon for its organization on August 30, 1862. The 104th deployed to Kentucky in September to block an anticipated offensive by the Confederates into Ohio at Cincinnati and then remained in the state for the nearly a year, guarding railroads and Union installations against Confederate raiders.

In August 1863, Greenawalt and the 104th moved into eastern Tennessee, where they took part in the capture and occupation of Knoxville. After what their unit history describes as a "brutal winter" in camp at Strawberry Plains, Tennessee, the regiment joined the campaign against Atlanta. It fought in northern Georgia at Dallas and Resaca and successfully cut the Atlanta and

Macon Railroad on July 30, 1864, interdicting the primary rebel supply route. The regiment's major battle up until that time had come on August 4–7 at Utoy Creek outside Atlanta. Greenawalt suffered a slight wound in the fight but returned to duty within a few days.

After securing Atlanta, the 104th marched into Tennessee to join Gen. George Thomas's defense against a counteroffensive led by Confederate general John Bell Hood. On November 30, the Confederates made a frontal attack against the Union defenses at Franklin, where the 104th, shouting "Remember Utoy," repulsed the major rebel assault. The Battle of Franklin produced six Medals of Honor for infantrymen of the 104th Ohio, including Greenawalt. All six were rewarded for their capture of enemy colors. Apparently the flag captured by Greenawalt was the highest-ranking, as it was from the rebel corps headquarters. His medal was presented on February 13, 1865.

The Union army fell back from Franklin to Nashville, where on December 15–16 it defeated the remainder of Hood's army, ending rebel occupation and influence in the region. From Nashville, the 104th made its way to the Eastern Theater for the Carolina Campaign, maneuvering north out of Charleston toward Richmond. When Gen. Robert E. Lee surrendered at Appomattox Court House in April 1865, the 104th was nearing Raleigh, North Carolina. The 104th and Greenawalt mustered out of active service on June 17, 1865.

During its three years of service, the 104th Ohio had an authorized manning of approximately 1,000 officers and enlisted men. About 1,740 men served during the war in the regiment, of which 3 officers and 46 enlisted men were killed or mortally wounded in combat and 4 officers and 130 enlisted men were lost to disease.

Greenawalt returned to Salem after his discharge and farmed outside the town of Alliance for the next twenty-nine years. His first marriage, to Jane A. Greenawalt, produced four children before her death in 1880. Greenawalt remarried, this time to Mary Jane Phillips, who survived Abraham. The Civil War hero retired in 1893 and moved to the nearby village of Damascus, where he lived until his death on October 24, 1922 (incorrectly listed as October 27 in most sources) at age eighty-eight. He is buried in the Alliance City Cemetery (Section H, Lot 88) with his first wife and two of their children. The John C. Fremont Post 729 of the Grand Army of the Republic in Alliance, of which Greenawalt was a member, along with officials of the local Methodist Episcopal Church, conducted the services.

After his death, the Alliance Historical Society took possession of Greenawalt's Medal of Honor. In the 1960s, the society loaned it to Mount Union College in Alliance for a military display. The medal was stolen and has never been recovered.

Gumpertz, Wolfe, and Simonhoff include Greenawalt in their lists of Jewish recipients of the Medal of Honor. Although Greenawalt was buried in a Protestant cemetery, there was a sizable Jewish population in Alliance during and after the Civil War. The Jewish population of the town did not, however, establish their Temple of Israel and cemetery until 1917. This is five years before Greenawalt's death, but there is no evidence that he was a practicing Jew at that time. Greenawalt, according to his obituary in the *Alliance Review*, worshiped at, and was a member of, the Damascus Methodist Episcopal Church (often misidentified as the Evangelical Lutheran Church).

Also, the name Greenawalt is not Jewish. Its origins are from the Anglo-Saxon name for a family who lived "as dwellers beside the green grassy hill or body of water." In Old English, it comes from the words "green" and "well." For these reasons Greenawalt is classified as a "topographic surname."

The Congressional Medal of Honor Society included Greenawalt on its list of Jewish recipients but recently removed his name, stating that "he was erroneously included in a list of Jewish recipients around 1910 and has been on every subsequent list afterwards, but more research has proven he should not be on the list." From that statement and his obituary, it is clear that Greenawalt did not claim to be a Jew at the time of his death. Nor did any of his family members. There is evidence, however, that while a soldier in the Civil War, he professed to being a Jew or coming from Jewish roots. Both Wolfe and Gumpertz, who were the experts at the time on Jewish veterans, include him on their list. For that reason he is included in this book as a "possible Jew."

22

David Linas Goodman,
Indian Wars, US Army

Company L, 8th US Cavalry Regiment

Lynx Creek, Arizona, October 14, 1869

Date Presented: March 3, 1870

CITATION:
Bravery in action.

DAVID GOODMAN has the briefest citation of all Jewish, or possibly any, Medal of Honor recipient. Little is known of the actions that earned him the award or of his life before or after his military service. He is one of about 300 recipients about whom the Congressional Medal of Honor Society states that much of his life has been "lost to history." Whether he was actually Jewish is a subject of debate.

It is known that Goodman was born on February 10, 1845, in Paxton, Massachusetts, to Eleages Goodwin of Columbus, Ohio, and Laura Lawless of Prescott, Massachusetts. There is no information available about David's early years other than census reports showing the family living in Shutesbury, Massachusetts, in 1850 and in Dana, Massachusetts, in 1860. On May 1, 1867, Goodman enlisted for a period of five years in the US Army at the Boston recruiting office. According to his enlistment records, he stood five feet five and one-half inches tall with a fair complexion, light hair, and gray eyes. He listed his civilian occupation as a farmer.

Upon his enlistment, Goodman went to California to join Troop L of the 8th Cavalry Regiment. The regiment had been initially established in 1866 with Troops L and M added on February 1, 1867, at Angel Island, California. Most of the enlistees were from the West Coast and the gold fields; their officers were almost all Civil War veterans. By the end of 1867, Troops B, I, K, and L were transferred to posts in Arizona Territory, where they performed escort and guard duty while also pursuing renegade Indians.

On March 3, 1870, Private Goodman, Pvt. John Raerick (also spelled Raerrick), and Pvt. John F. Rowalt received Medals of Honor for their actions the previous October 14. Goodman's citation states, "Bravery in action," while Raerick's and Rowalt's state, "Gallantry in action with Indians at Lyry Creek, Arizona."

Although the three obviously would not been awarded their medals had they not performed bravely, there are several problems with the citations and with the descriptions of what actually occurred. The only document from the time to survive is the post return of Fort Whipple, Arizona, for the month of October 1869. In the Record of Events section, a hand-written statements says, "Fourteen men belonging to Companies D and L, 8th Cavalry left post October 14th in pursuit of a band of Indians who were reported in the area of Lynx Creek—but after thoroughly scouring the country in that vicinity were unable to find any fresh Indian signs—Returned to post October 16th –no results—Distance marched 66 miles."

Although the document properly spells Lynx Creek, the Medal of Honor citations misspell the location as Lyry Creek. It was not until December 20, 2017, that the Department of the Army officially changed the spelling to Lynx. As for the slight difference between the wording of Goodman's citation and that of his two fellow cavalrymen, as well as the Fort Whipple post return making no mention of the action, there is no explanation other than being "lost in history." It is possible that the action occurred on a different date or that the recorder did not have the correct information—or just failed to accurately note the incident. An entry in the November 1869 Fort Whipple post record states that a cavalry patrol killed two Indians in a fight, with "David Goodman slightly wounded," but the entry includes no exact date or other information.

The next year, L Troop moved to New Mexico, where Goodman appears in the Mora County Census of 1870. He was discharged from the army on May 15, 1872, at Fort Union, New Mexico, because of "expiration of service." The 1900 census shows Goodman living in Orange Township, Massachusetts, where, according to the *Orange Enterprise and Journal* of the time, he worked as a foreman in the New Home Sewing Machine plant before establishing a livery stable. He must have been successful because the same newspaper reported on May 9, 1890, the following news item: "At the auction of Ballou Bros. at the Contre, last week, horses sold from $15 to $715. David Goodman of Orange bought the noted stock horse for $715."

On an unknown date he married Abbie F. Stone. According to his death certificate, Goodman died of apoplexy at age sixty-two on April 19, 1907, at his residence at 48 West Main Street in Orange. He is buried in the Orange Central Cemetery. His wife, Abbie, who died in 1936, is buried at his side. Other than their names and birth and death dates on their joint headstone, the only other engraving is the Masonic Square and Compass of Freemasonry. There is no known photograph or other image of Goodman.

Nothing in Goodman's records note his religious affiliation. The Congressional Medal of Honor Society does not include Goodman on its list of Jewish American medal recipients. Many websites and other lists do include Goodman on their rosters of Jewish Americans who earned the Medal of Honor—but without any references validating their claim. Although there are Jews with the surname of Goodman, the name is of Anglo-Scottish origins. Goodman's mother's maiden surname of Lawless is also of Anglo origins. For these reasons, David Goodman is included in this list only as a possible Jew.

★★★

23

Jacob Trautman,
Indian Wars, US Army

Company I, 7th US Cavalry Regiment
Wounded Knee Creek, South Dakota, December 29, 1890
Date Presented: March 27, 1891

CITATION:
Killed a hostile Indian at close quarters, and, although entitled to retirement from service, remained to the close of the campaign.

JACOB TRAUTMAN fought as a cavalryman in the Civil War and Indian Wars as he advanced in rank from private to 1st sergeant. He earned his Medal of Honor in the US Army's final battle against Native Americans at Wounded Knee Creek, South Dakota, when he was only days away from retirement. Born sometime in 1840 in an unidentified town in Bavaria, Germany (often misidentified as Hamburg), to Jacob and Margaret Trautman, the young Jacob immigrated with his parents to America, but just when is unknown. Nothing is available about his youth or his education.

The first known official record of Trautman is his enlistment for three years in Company L of the 5th Pennsylvania Volunteer Cavalry on August 9, 1861, in Pittsburgh, Pennsylvania. The "Company Descriptive Book" states that the enlistee stood five feet six inches tall with a fair complexion, blue eyes, and brown hair. His civilian occupation was listed as that of laborer. According to a letter Trautman wrote to the US Army's adjutant general on July 18, 1891, requesting that he be placed on the retired rolls, he was "Discharged January 24, 1864 (at Portsmouth, Virginia), and reenlisted to serve in Company L, 5th

Pennsylvania Volunteer Cavalry until June, 1865, when the regiment was consolidated with the 3rd Pennsylvania Volunteer Cavalry. Discharged August 7, 1865 from Company E, 3rd Pennsylvania Volunteer Cavalry."

Other than his promotions to corporal on July 5, 1864, and to sergeant on March 1, 1865, there is no further documentation of his individual Civil War service. Records do reveal that the 5th Pennsylvania Cavalry primarily performed security and reconnaissance duties in the vicinity of Washington, DC, before joining the Siege and Battle of Petersburg and then participating in the Appomattox Campaign, which concluded with the surrender of Gen. Robert E. Lee's Army of Northern Virginia at Appomattox Court House in April 1865. During the war the 5th Regiment lost a total of 293 men, including 1 officer and 76 enlisted men killed or mortally wounded and 6 officers and 210 enlisted men who died of disease.

Trautman returned to Pennsylvania after his discharge but soon found that he missed the action, adventure, and comradery, as well as job security, of being a soldier. On August 22, 1867, he enlisted at Pittsburgh for three years in Company F of the 4th US Infantry Regiment—established in 1792, making it one of the oldest infantry regiments in the army. Upon the completion of his enlistment, Trautman received an honorable discharged as a private at Fort Laramie, Wyoming Territory, on August 22, 1870. Under the "Character" section of his discharge, his commander noted that he was "a good soldier."

The future hero made his way to Cincinnati, Ohio, where he once again decided to return to the army. On December 21, 1870, he volunteered for Company A of the 19th US Infantry Regiment and five years later received another honorable discharge as a private at Fort Dodge, Kansas, with the "Character" statement of "Very good." He served most of his time with the 19th Infantry during the Reconstruction period in New Orleans and Shreveport, Louisiana, before the regiment's transfer west to counter rising Indian aggression.

Trautman returned to Pittsburgh, but his stay was brief. Once again he was drawn back to the army, this time to a longtime home. On January 4, 1876, Trautman joined Company I of the 7th US Cavalry Regiment. By the time he completed his enlistment five years later, he had advanced in rank from private to 1st sergeant of his company. This rapid rise in rank resulted from Trautman's experience and leadership as well as his unit's combat against the Native Americans, for Company I was one of five companies annihilated at the Little Bighorn on June 26, 1876. History failed to record why Trautman was not with his unit that fateful day.

In all likelihood, he remained at the regiment's headquarters at Fort Abraham Lincoln, Dakota Territory, for administrative or medical reasons, or perhaps he might have been detached to one of the 7th Regiment's other two columns during the fight. Whatever the reason for his absence, he rose in rank quickly, as experienced leaders were needed to reconstitute the company after the Battle of the Little Bighorn.

After his five-year enlistment was completed, 1st Sergeant Trautman was discharged at Fort Totten, Dakota Territory, on January 3, 1881, and reenlisted for another five-year tour with Company I the next day. On January 3, 1886, Trautman was honorably discharged at Fort Meade, Dakota Territory, and once again reenlisted for five more years on January 4.

In a report that was a part of Trautman's retirement records, the commanding officer of Company I wrote on August 30, 1891, that the 1st sergeant had "participated in campaign against hostile Nez Perce Indians in 1877; was present in the fight at Canyon Creek, Montana Territory on September 13, 1877. Also in the campaign against hostile Cheyennes in Nebraska in 1878."

On December 29, 1890, the 7th Cavalry was sent to disarm a band of 350 Sioux Indians—230 warriors, including some veterans of the Battle of the Little Bighorn, and 120 women and children—at Wounded Knee Creek on the Lakota Pine Ridge Reservation in South Dakota. Government officials were concerned that the Indians might break out of the reservation to occupy some of the tribal members' lost land. This concern was based on the Indians' Ghost Dance movement that promised that Ghost Shirts would protect their wearers from soldier bullets.

In a cavalryman's effort to take a rifle from one of the warriors, the weapon discharged and a pitched battle began. In the ensuing fight, more than 150 warriors, women, and children—including their chief, Spotted Elk—were killed and another 51 wounded. Later, near the end of the twentieth century, white and Indian activist groups began declaring the fight was not a battle but rather a "massacre," some claiming that the 7th Cavalry was out for revenge for Little Bighorn. In a time of acute political correctness in 1990, both houses of the US Congress passed resolutions expressing "deep regret" for the incident.

What exactly occurred at Wounded Knee has been lost to history and obscured by the fog of war. It is difficult to accept, however, that the battle was a massacre because of the fact that twenty-five cavalrymen were killed in the fight and another thirty-nine wounded—six of whom subsequently died of their wounds. For their efforts to disarm the Indians, many of whom erroneously believing their Ghost Shirts would protect them, and to protect their fellow cavalrymen, twenty members of the 7th Cavalry earned the Medal of Honor at Wounded Knee.

Included was 1st Sergeant Trautman. His recommendation for the award states,

> Commanding Officer Troop I, 7th Cavalry recommends this man for a Medal of Honor for distinguished conduct at Wounded Knee, South Dakota, December 29, 1890 as follows: The soldier distinguished himself under the personal observation of the troop commander by the coolness and courage displayed throughout that action and especially by his conduct in killing an Indian at close quarters who would have probably killed others of the command; Trautman's term of service expired while in the field and he could have been placed on the retired list, but he preferred to reenlist and remain until the campaign had ended. Approved by the Regimental Adjutant (in the absence of the Regt. Comdr.) and by the Dept. Comdr. The Adjutant adds that 1st Sergt. Trautman's action on the day specified was the subject of common talk and admiration throughout the command.

On January 3, 1891, less than a week after the Battle of Wounded Knee, Trautman completed his enlistment and the next day reenlisted at Pine Ridge Agency for the final time. His Medal of Honor was awarded the following March 27. Trautman transferred from the active to the retired rolls of the US Army on August 3 at Fort Riley, Kansas. He returned to Pittsburgh, where he resided until his death at age fifty-eight from a cerebral hemorrhage at his home at 21 Carson Street on November 7, 1898. There is no record of his ever marrying or having children, nor is there any photograph or other image of him. He is buried in the city's South Side Cemetery (Soldiers Plot, Grave 148).

Trautman is included on many lists of Jewish Medal of Honor recipients. However, none provide verification. He might have been included on early lists by fellow veterans who knew him and were aware that he was a Jew. Or perhaps he was erroneously entered on an early roll of recipients, and the mistake was merely repeated over and over. There is no record of Trautman's religious preference in any of his official documents.

The only bit of evidence of Trautman's religion or ethnic origins is found on VA Form 40-1330, Application for Standard Government Monument, submitted by Wesley R. Slusher on August 6, 1991. On the form Slusher states that he is not related to Trautman. A Latin cross is checked in the column "Desired Emblem Reflective of One's Belief." The application was made during an effort in the latter part of the twentieth century to mark all recipients' graves with a Medal of Honor headstone. There had been no previous such marker on Trautman's grave. The person who submitted the form had no information on his religious beliefs and likely requested the Latin cross as a guess rather than information from an informed source.

Because of the lack of verifiable information, the Congressional Medal of Honor Society does not include Trautman on its list of confirmed or unconfirmed Jewish recipients. However, because Trautman is included in many lists of Jewish Medal of Honor recipients, he is included in this study as possibly Jewish.

★★★

24

William F. Zion,
Boxer Rebellion, US Marine Corps

USMC Detachment USS *Newark*

Peking, China, July 21–August 17, 1900

Date Presented: December 11, 1901

CITATION:

In the presence of the enemy during the battle of Peking, China, 21 July to 17 August 1900. Throughout this period, Zion distinguished himself by meritorious conduct.

WILLIAM F. ZION served his country in both the US Marine Corps and the US Army with bravery on the battlefield; yet he died a mysterious death. Born on October 23, 1872, in Knightstown, Indiana, to Thomas Jefferson and Mary C. Zion, William grew up as the youngest of four children who included two brothers and a sister. His early history is unknown. Census data show the family living in Knightstown in 1880.

By the late 1880s, the Zions had moved to Indianapolis, where the city directories for 1887–1890 show the elder Zion employed as a "traveling agent" for Wiles, Coffin & Company at 267 E. Market Street. William is listed as working for the same company at the same address as a "checkman"—meaning he worked as a timekeeper and payroll clerk.

By the time Zion was in his twenties, he had become bored with the life of a clerk in the Midwest and had made his way to San Francisco, California. His later enlistment papers state his occupation as "motorman," likely as an operator on the city's famed cable car system. Operating a trolley car must have lacked sufficient excitement and adventure, for Zion enlisted in the Marine Corps at Mare Island on July 21, 1899. The papers describe him as fair-skinned with auburn hair and blue eyes.

Older than most enlistees at age twenty-six, Zion quickly adapted to military life. Soon he was assigned to the marine detachment aboard the USS *Newark*—the last of the "mixed cruisers" launched in 1890 that could be propelled either by sail or steam—which had just arrived in San Francisco after having cruised in the North Atlantic, in the Caribbean, and off South America. His commanding officer was Capt. Newt Hall.

The *Newark* sailed to Hong Kong, the Philippines, and Japan before heading for China in May 1900 after the outbreak of the Boxer Rebellion. Boxers, so named for their practice of gymnastics and other physical exercises and formally known as the Society of Righteous and Harmonious Fists, had rebelled against the Chinese government earlier in the year because of their opposition to foreign presence and influence on their country. The Chinese government, led by Tzu Hsi, the empress dowager of the Manchu Dynasty, initially opposed the Boxers.

On June 19, Tzu Hsi changed her mind and demanded that foreigners leave the country while she also praised "the brave followers of the Boxers." Despite this shift, the United States stood by its Open Door policy for China, as did the delegations of Austria-Hungry, France, Germany, Great Britain, Italy, Japan, and Russia. All refused to evacuate as their diplomatic delegations, missionaries, and business personnel, as well as Christian Chinese, retreated into a walled area in Peking that housed the residences of foreign diplomats.

Rescue groups from all eight countries rushed to Peking to aid the besieged legation. Among the first to arrive were Captain Hall and 23 marines, including Zion, from the *Newark* who joined 26 marines from the USS *Oregon* and 350 military personnel from the other legation countries. On June 18 the Chinese government declared a state of war and two days later began firing artillery and small arms into the foreign compound.

Zion and his fellow marines resisted against great odds. Although the Boxers were fierce fighters, they had little military training or adequate leadership. The exact details of Zion's heroism have been lost to history other than the dates of his actions and his citation, which states that he "distinguished himself by meritorious conduct."

However, in an interview shortly before his death, Zion said,

For five days and nights we fought without rest, without any sleep, and with hardly time to eat. It was the hardest place that I have even been in, and before it was over with most of us gave up hope of ever getting out alive. Most of the fighting at first was with Boxers, and we made little excursions to rescue refugees, the converted Chinese. About June 20, however, the imperial army turned against us, and then we had to fight almost constantly. We had very little food, and the water was really not fit to drink. We didn't take time to boil it, though. We hardly had our belts off during the entire time we were there, and when we slept, our rifles were in our hands. We became so used to having our rifles that we never thought of putting them down and walking away from them.

Over the next month and a half, more than 20,000 allied troops landed in China and began moving to rescue the Peking legation. The international relief column reached Peking on August 24 and quickly broke the siege. On September 7 the Chinese government signed the Boxer Protocol, which provided for the execution of officials who had supported the Boxers, provisions for the future stationing of international forces in Peking, and a payment of what is today equal to $333 million in silver as well as taxes over the next thirty-nine years to pay for the expenses of the Allies.

During their defense of the legation, seven of the forty-eight enlisted marines were killed. Nine enlisted marines were wounded as was one of their two officers as well as the attached naval assistant surgeon.

Zion and his fellow marines returned to their ships shortly after the signing of the Boxer Protocol and departed for the Philippines. From there the *Newark* sailed to Hong Kong, Ceylon, and the Suez Canal and on to its new port in Boston. On July 19, 1901, the Department of the Navy published orders awarding the Medal of Honor to Zion, but it was not actually awarded until the *Newark* was in port on December 11.

Shortly after the relief of the Peking Legation, US Minister to China E. H. Conger wrote Sec. of State John Hay, "To our Marines fell the most difficult and dangerous portion of the defense by reason of our proximity to the great city wall, and the main city gates over which the large guns were planted. Our legation, with the position which we held on the wall, was the key to the whole situation."

American missionaries in the legation published a resolution stating, "The Americans who have been besieged in Peking desire to express their hearty appreciation of the courage, fidelity, and patriotism of the American Marines, to whom we so largely owe our salvation. By their bravery in holding an almost untenable position on the city wall in the face of overwhelming numbers, and in cooperating in driving the Chinese from a position of great strength, they made all foreigners in Peking their debtors, and have gained for themselves an honorable name among the heroes of their country."

In Boston the *Newark* went into dry dock for repairs and refitting before taking up station in the West Indies and then returning to Boston in 1904. Zion, because of his bravery exhibited in Peking and for his leadership abilities, advanced in rank to corporal in 1902 and then to sergeant the following year. On July 15, 1904, Zion received a general court martial that reduced him in rank back to private. The basis of the trial remains a mystery, as no records about the charges have survived. They must not have been too severe, for Zion was granted an honorable discharge from the Marine Corps two weeks later in Boston on July 29.

Whatever brought on the court martial and its results apparently affected Zion's feelings for the Marine Corps, but it did not dampen his enthusiasm for the military life. A week after his discharge, he enlisted as a private in the US Army on August 5. Zion served in various infantry assignments and rose up the ranks, receiving "excellent" character ratings. With the outbreak of World War I and the expansion of the US Armed Services, the army promoted Zion to 2nd lieutenant on July 8, 1917, and to 1st lieutenant the following February.

Likely, because of his age and not wanting to risk a Medal of Honor recipient in further combat, the army assigned Zion duty in the United States. He served in the headquarters of War Prison Barracks No. 2 at Fort Oglethorpe near Chattanooga, Tennessee, a prison established in March 1917 as a confinement facility for captured German naval personnel.

On the morning of March 25, 1919, Zion died of a bullet wound to the head. An investigation failed to resolve whether the fatal shot was self-inflicted or an accident while Zorn was cleaning his pistol. Family and friends believed in the latter explanation. Obituaries in the two Chattanooga newspapers reported that Zion had many friends in the area and that he had served in China. Interestingly, neither mentioned that he had received the Medal of Honor. Zion never had children of his own but at the time of his death was married and had several stepchildren. He is buried in Chattanooga National Cemetery (Section U, Grave 40). There is no known photograph or other image of Zion.

In 1981 American Legion Post 152 of Knightstown, Indiana, dedicated a monument to Zion. It is located on Washington Street in the Veterans Garden of Memories opposite the town square.

Zion's name is on nearly every list of Jewish Medal of Honor recipients, several of which cite Sydney G. Gumpertz, author of *The Jewish Legion of Valor*, who classified Zion as a Jew. There is no notation in his official records that confirm or refute this claim. Neither his headstone nor those of his parents or his paternal grandparents contain any religious symbols whatsoever. Perhaps they came from Jewish roots but had long ceased practicing the religion; or maybe they had no religious background, including Judaism, at all. The most obvious evidence of Zion's heritage is from his name. Zion is from the name of a citadel that was in the center of Jerusalem and is also used to refer to a Jewish homeland and to heaven.

The Congressional Medal of Honor Society does not include Zion on its roster of Jewish American recipients. Neither do they include him on their list of "may have been Jewish; unconfirmed." For these reasons Zion is included in the "Possibly Jewish" section of this book.

★★★

25

Louis Clinton Mosher,
Philippine Insurrection, US Army

Philippine Scouts

Jolo, Philippine Islands, June 11, 1911

Date Presented: March 16, 1914

CITATION:
Voluntarily entered a cleared space within 20 yards of the Moro trenches under a furious fire from them and carried a wounded soldier of his company to safety at the risk of his own life.

LOUIS MOSHER served for thirty years in the US Army, rising through the enlisted ranks to be appointed a commissioned officer and to earn the Medal of Honor. The future hero, who received his medal while fighting Moro warriors during the Philippine Insurrection, entered life on July 14, 1883, in Westport, Massachusetts. His parents, Edmund A. and Abigail F. Mosher, were both natives of Massachusetts; his father was born in Dartmouth and his mother in Portsmouth.

Little is known of Mosher's childhood other than he apparently grew up in the Smith Mill section of Dartmouth. He was working as a motorman for the local trolley system when, on November 9, 1901, he enlisted in the US Army at New Bedford, Massachusetts, for a period of three years. His enlistment papers note that he stood five feet seven and three quarters inches tall with blue eyes, brown hair, and a fair complexion. Although his enlistment officer was from the 17th US Infantry Regiment, Mosher soon joined the 6th US Cavalry Regiment fighting rebels in the Philippines before the unit's transfer to Fort Meade, South Dakota, in 1903. Assigned to the regiment's Company K, Mosher advanced in rank to corporal and then to sergeant.

Upon the completion of his enlistment on November 8, 1904, Mosher returned to Massachusetts, where he moved in with his brother Charles at 75 South Main in Brockton. Mosher soon tired of civilian life, and on November 1, 1905, in Boston he again enlisted as a private in the US Army. Assigned to border duty with Company C of the 1st US Cavalry Regiment at Fort Clark, Texas, Mosher once more advanced in rank to sergeant. The 1st Cavalry moved to San Francisco to assist in the aftermath of the 1906 earthquake and then returned to Texas. On October 7, 1907, Mosher was honorably discharged so he could again reenlist the next day for three more years. His reenlistment papers note, "Indelible or permanent marks found on the person of a recruit" as "tattoo letters 'LCM' and wreath bracelet and rose on right wrist, clasped hands and heart front left forearm, coat of arms and bracelet with head of man back of left forearm, and star on thumb."

In 1908 the 1st Cavalry transferred back to the Philippines, where it performed mostly garrison duty at Fort Stotsenburg. When the regiment prepared to return to the United States in early 1910, Mosher elected to remain in the Philippines with the Philippine Scouts, an army unit of Filipino Americans formed in 1901 to combat rebels. Known as Moros, these local Muslims, who resided mostly in the southern Philippines, were fierce warriors who fought with both modern weapons and edged machete-like knives. The most skilled and dedicated of these soldiers were the Juramentado, who attacked Filipino police, US soldiers, and Philippine Scouts. For these acts, they expected to achieve martyrdom upon their death.

Brig. Gen. John J. Pershing—future leader of US forces in Europe during World War I—served as the military governor of Moro Province from 1909 to 1913, which included Mosher's tour. Although there is no evidence that Pershing ordered the practice, the Americans and Philippine Scouts took unusually harsh measures in combating the Moros. In his autobiography Pershing wrote, "[The] juramentado attacks were materially reduced in number by a practice the army had already adopted, one that the Mohammadans held in abhorrence. The bodies were publicly buried in the same grave with a dead pig. It was not pleasant to have to take such measures but the prospect of going to hell instead of heaven sometimes deterred the would-be assassins."

The Philippine Scouts were mostly led by American officers. As a part of his transfer to the Scouts, the army promoted Mosher to the rank of 2nd lieutenant in the infantry on February 4, 1910. For more than a year Mosher and his Scouts patrolled the islands of the southern Philippines in pursuit of the Moros. On July 11, 1913, Mosher's Scouts encountered an entrenched Moro unit on Bagsak Mountain on Jolo Island.

A year later, on July 3, a Chicago newspaper, *The Day Book*, wrote about Mosher and the battle. The newspaper described Mosher as a "simple soldier" and "a first class fighting man." The article continued, "He speaks but little. He never swears, nor drinks, smokes, nor chews. His fellows have considered him a Sunday School model, rather than devil-may-care type of hero."

About the fight that led to Mosher's Medal of Honor, the newspaper reported,

> A detachment of the Philippine Scouts, campaigning in the mountains of Jolo, were being desperately opposed by a strong body of Moros. American troops have never anywhere encountered more wicked and fanatical fighters than the Moros. They are the Mohammedans. They would rather be killed than not, for death in battle means reward in Heaven to them. But they aim to kill as many 'infidels' as they can before they fall.
>
> Armed with modern rifles, and with their own nasty snaky-bladed kris, they go into battle with a wild elation that augurs ill for the enemy. They bind their arms and legs tightly with reeds to impede the flow of blood when they are wounded, and so fight fiercely on after other soldiers would have fainted from loss of blood.
>
> It was almost into the trenches of the fiercest band of Moros left in the Philippines that Lieutenant Mosher dashed on his courageous mission.
>
> A private in Mosher's company had fallen in a repulsed attack upon the strong Moro position on the side of Bagsak Mountain. The man was badly wounded and helpless. The Moros were firing furiously across the open space in which he lay.
>
> Suddenly, Lieutenant Mosher leaped from the American lines and charged at full speed across the bullet-swept clearing. It is hard to say whether Mosher's own men, or the Moros, were more astonished at the fool recklessness of the act. Their paralyzed amazement was marked by a sudden lull in the firing. Then a perfect hurricane of shots burst from the Moro trenches. And right through the heart of the storm of bullets ran Lieutenant Mosher, bare-headed, unarmed, and never flinching, toward the fallen private.
>
> Mosher ran up to the wounded man, who was writhing in pain, shouldered him, and turned calmly, but speedily back toward safety.

The article concluded by stating that not only did Mosher's bravery save a man's life but also his daring had so confused the Moros that the engagement had been won by the Scouts. Over the next week, the article was reprinted in newspapers across the United States.

After the battle Mosher's immediate reward was that of every infantryman in combat. He continued the mission, remained in the field, and fought on against the enemy. However, when his leaders learned of his bravery, they promoted him to 1st lieutenant and recommended him for the Medal of Honor. It took nearly four years, during which time Mosher continued to lead his Scouts against the Moros, before the War Department published, on March 16, 1914, General Order No. 18. The order announced the approval of the Medal of Honor for Mosher. It also stated that, because Mosher was still stationed in the Philippines—making it impracticable for the president, as commander in chief, to present the medal—Maj. Gen. Thomas H. Barry, the commanding general of the Philippine Department of the Army, was to make the presentation as the president's representative.

Mosher remained in the army after his duties in the Philippines and served mostly at various posts in California. In the army's reduction of force in the early 1920s, Mosher reverted to his precommissioning rank of sergeant and then rose to the rank of master sergeant. An article in the *New York Times* on March 24, 1928, noted that Mosher, assigned to the 11th US Cavalry Regiment at Camp Hearn, California, was one of two enlisted Medal of Honor recipients still on active duty. The March 17, 1930, issue of the *Oakland Tribune* reported that Mosher had transferred from the Presidio at San Francisco to help train the Nevada National Guard.

The Philippine Scout hero retired from the army on November 28, 1932. An article in the *New York Times* noted his retirement, reporting that, with his departure from the army, only one enlisted man with the Medal of Honor remained on active duty.

There is no record of Mosher ever having children, but he did marry Florence Vivian Hostrawser. Florence died in San Francisco on April 4, 1958. Mosher died five months later on September 29 at Letterman Hospital. Both are buried in San Francisco National Cemetery (Section NA, Plots 1408 and 1409). Florence's daughter and Mosher's stepdaughter, Florence Barrett, made the burial arrangements and submitted the application for his Medal of Honor headstone.

Although Mosher appears on many lists of Jewish Medal of Honor recipients, there is no direct evidence to support the claim. Many Jews are named Mosher; so are many non-Jews. There is a possibility that Mosher, his parents, or other relatives were Jews but had left the faith. The Congressional Medal of Honor Society does not include Mosher in its Jewish recipients list or on its list of possible but unconfirmed Jews. When Florence Barrett requested her stepfather's headstone, she requested a Christian emblem. Her mother's headstone also has the Christian cross. According to his death records, Mosher's burial services were performed by the post chaplain, not the post rabbi. It is also notable that Mosher's early enlistment records indicate that he had multiple tattoos, a practice that goes against the general tenants of Judaism.

★★★

26

Edouard Victor Michel Izac,
World War I, US Navy

USS *President Lincoln*

North Atlantic and Germany, May 21–November 11, 1918

Date Presented: November 11, 1920

CITATION:

When the U. S. S. President Lincoln was attacked and sunk by the German submarine U-90, on May 21, 1918, Lt. Izac was captured and held as a prisoner on board the U-90 until the return of the submarine to Germany, when he was confined in the prison camp. During his stay on the U-90 he obtained information of the movements of German submarines which was so important that he was determined to escape, with a view to making this information available to the U. S. and Allied Naval authorities. In attempting to carry out this plan, he jumped through the window of a rapidly moving train at the imminent risk of death, not only from the nature of the act itself but from the fire of the armed German soldiers who were guarding him. Having been recaptured and reconfined, Lt. Izac made a second and successful attempt to escape, breaking his way through barbed-wire fences and deliberately drawing the fire of the armed guards in the hope of permitting others to escape during the confusion. He made his way through the mountains of southwestern Germany, having only raw vegetables for food, and at the end, swam the Rhine River during the night in the immediate vicinity of German sentries.

EDOUARD IZAC is the only US Navy officer to receive the Medal of Honor for his service in World War I. His story—as torpedoed sailor, German captive, and escapee from a prisoner of war camp—is unique among medal recipients of all conflicts.

Born the youngest of nine children to Balthazar and Mathilda Geuth Isaacs on December 18, 1891, in Cresco, Iowa, the future naval hero grew up speaking German as well as English in his home, as his parents both had German roots. His father, who had immigrated to the United States from his native Alsace-Lorraine, had grown up with that language. Because Americans had difficulties pronouncing Izac, Balthazar had changed the family name to Isaacs upon arrival in America. His mother, Mathilda, although born in Philadelphia, was the daughter of immigrants from Baden-Wurttemberg.

Edouard attended elementary school at the Catholic School of Assumption in Cresco and then attended high school in South St. Paul, Minnesota. From the time he was a boy, Isaacs wanted to attend the US Naval Academy and become a naval officer. Although academically and physically qualified, Isaacs could not secure an appointment from his Republican congressman because his father was a staunch Democrat. As result, Isaacs lived with a brother in Chicago and worked there for several years before entering Werntz Preparatory in Annapolis, Maryland, near the academy. His study there finally earned him an appointment as a member of the Class of 1915.

Upon graduation, Isaacs married Agnes Cabell, the daughter of army general De Rosey Carroll Cabell, a veteran of the Boxer Rebellion and Pershing's expedition into Mexico. Isaacs' first assignment was aboard the battleship USS *Florida*, where he earned promotion from ensign to lieutenant junior grade. In July 1917 he transferred to the Naval Transport Service and boarded the troop transport USS *President Lincoln* on October 18 for its maiden voyage across the Atlantic Ocean.

Isaacs made five routine round-trip voyages to Europe as the ship's officer in charge of its two six-inch guns over the next eight months. On his sixth trip, however, three torpedoes from the German submarine U-90 struck the *President Lincoln* on May 31, 1918, and quickly sent it to the bottom. Most of the crew and passengers, including Isaacs, successfully abandoned ship and climbed aboard lifeboats. The U-90 captain surfaced in order to capture an American officer to confirm his "kill" and to eventually turn over to German intelligence for interrogation. Isaac was taken aboard the German submarine as a prisoner of war. Not revealing his fluency in German and acting somewhat addled from his ordeal, he remained a captive in the U-90 for the next three weeks, enduring an attack by an American destroyer that failed to damage the submarine. All the while Isaacs gathered information on the operation and procedures of the U-90 in hopes he might get the information back to the Allies.

Isaacs made his first escape attempt by trying to jump overboard while the submarine was on the surface and nearing shore. Strong hands of his captors grabbed him before he could jump. Then when the U-90 finally put into port in northern Germany at Kiel, Isaacs was put on a prisoner train bound for a camp at Karlsruhe. Isaacs climbed through a bathroom window, and when the train slowed for a curve, he jumped, spraining an ankle when he landed and hindering him from outrunning guards who came in pursuit from the now-stopped train.

After a thorough beating, Isaacs was put back on the train and delivered to the POW camp. He quickly planned another escape with fellow prisoners for the Fourth of July but was thwarted when additional guards were posted at their escape point. Yet another plan failed when the camp commandant intercepted a letter from a fellow prisoner to his girlfriend about the escape. The Germans placed Isaacs and several other prisoners aboard another train for a more secure camp at Villengen. En route Isaacs once again jumped from the train, only to be stunned and bloodied when he landed on a parallel track. He was returned to the train.

Despite his injuries, Isaacs immediately began plans for another escape attempt when he arrived at Villengen. Near midnight on October 6, Isaacs short-circuited the camp's lighting system and electrified fence with a stolen wire so that he and eleven other POWs could escape into the night. Once outside, they broke into two-man teams and began their 150-mile journey westward toward neutral Switzerland. Isaacs and his partner outdistanced their pursuers by spreading pepper stolen from the camp mess hall on their path to throw the guard's dogs off their scent.

For a week, Isaacs and his companion walked through the night and hid during the day, surviving by eating raw vegetables taken from farmers' fields. They were so weak when they reached the Rhine River at the German-Swiss border that they barely managed to make it to freedom on the other side. A helpful farmer fed Isaacs and turned him over to Swiss authorities, who delivered him to the American Legation in Bern. On October 16 the legation issued Isaacs an Emergency Passport with the statement that he had "[e]scaped from Germany where he was held as a prisoner of war. This passport issued at request of the Military Attaché."

American intelligence officers debriefed Isaacs after his escape. Their findings—in the form of a memo from the commander of US Naval Forces Operating in European Waters to the secretary of the navy, titled "Sinking of the USS *President Lincoln*" and dated November 4—detailed how the U-90 had sunk the ship and included recommendations on how future attacks could be avoided. Although the war ended before the recommendations could be implemented, the ideas of convoy speed and zig-zagging would be adapted a quarter century later in World War II. The navy deemed the information so important that it did not declassify the memo until 1990.

Isaacs immediately departed for the United States with the purpose of providing additional information about German submarine operations to the Navy Department. Writing en route and upon his arrival in Washington, DC, he submitted his "Report on Imprisonment in Germany and Escape Therefrom" to the secretary of the navy on November 13, 1918. By this time, however, the armistice ending the war had been signed and German submarines no longer posed a danger. Over the next months, Isaacs expanded his report into a full-length book about his capture, imprisonment, and escape, which was published as *Prisoner of the U-90* the next year.

The governments of Italy and Montenegro honored Isaacs with medals. On November 11, 1920, Asst. Sec. of the Navy Franklin Delano Roosevelt presented the Medal of Honor to Isaacs in a ceremony at the Washington Navy Yard. A year later, because his wounds incurred while a prisoner had not completely healed, Isaac retired from the navy. He and his family relocated to San Diego, California, where he became a journalist. In 1924, Isaacs visited his father's relatives in Alsace and decided to change his name to the one that rightfully belonged to him. Isaacs legally became Izac in 1925. Some accounts incorrectly claim that Izac changed his name when he entered the Naval Academy. The navy advanced him to the rank of lieutenant commander on the retired rolls in 1936.

Izac became an active member of the American Legion, worked on various local issues, and continued as a journalist. In 1934 he ran unsuccessfully for the US Congress. Two years later he won the election and then served for a decade in Congress, his tenure as a congressman spanning all of World War II. He also served as a delegate to the 1940 and 1944 Democratic National Conventions.

At the conclusion of conflict in Europe and at the request of Gen. Dwight D. Eisenhower, Izac and eleven other congressmen and senators traveled to Germany to inspect the liberated concentrated camps at Buchenwald, Nordhausen Buchenwald, and Dachau. Izac coauthored the report of the trip, titled "Atrocities and Other Conditions in Concentration Camps in Germany" and published on May 15, 1945.

Not reelected in 1946, Izac retired to a farm near Gordonsville, Virginia, were he raised purebred cattle and engaged in the timber industry. In the early 1960s the Izacs retired from the farm and moved to Bethesda, Maryland. Izac showed that he had no fear of going back to sea as he and Agnes made many cruises around the world and, on one occasion, visited Bethlehem on Christmas Eve.

His wife died in 1975. Because of failing health, he moved in with his daughter, Suzanne Smallwood Quinlan, in Fairfax, Virginia, in 1987. In a letter to friends on December 28, 1987, Quinlan wrote that her father continued to be called "Chum" or "Chummy" by family and friends, reporting, "He remains very lucid much of the time, recalls fond memories and enjoys a cigar after dinner each night, with a happy hour before dinner!" Despite his age, he enjoyed raising tomatoes and cucumbers in his daughter's backyard garden.

Izac, the last living World War I Medal of Honor recipient, died on December 18, 1990, of congestive heart failure; he was ninety-nine years old to the day. He is buried in Arlington National Cemetery (Section 3, Lot 4222-16) in Washington, DC, and his wife and a son are buried at his side. Izac's Medal of Honor is on display at the Naval Historical Center in the Washington Navy Yard.

In addition to his great heroism and longtime service to his country, Izac also serves as an excellent example of the errors in the narratives of many recipients of the Medal of Honor—especially considering that he lived until near the end of the twentieth century. His given name of Michel is often misspelled as Michael. Many sources, including the US Congress and Willard Scott, weatherman on NBC's *Today* show, honored him for his 100th birthday when in fact he was only 98. Before replacement, his date of death was incorrect on his headstone. The obituaries in many newspapers, including the *Washington Post*, *New York Times*, and *Stars and Stripes*, also reported his age incorrectly at the time of his death.

Although Izac is listed as a Jewish American on nearly all lists of recipients, with the exception of the Congressional Medal of Honor Society, there is overwhelming evidence that he did not practice the religion. At the time of his death, he was a member of the Roman Catholic Church of the Little Flower in Bethesda. Suzanne Quinlan wrote in her letter of 1987 that her father "enjoys going to early morning mass with us, picking out our Christmas tree, etc."

An interview with Izac that appeared in the *Washington Post* about the same time stated, "By the ash tray on the table between us were two shallow dishes each containing a rosary, and in the center was a colored figurine of Christ with his arms stretched out in a way of welcoming. . . . There were a few other clues that Izac is religious although this was not discussed."

Izac's burial services were held at St. Leo's Catholic Church in Fairfax, and his headstone has the Christian cross symbol.

The only indication of Izac's being of Jewish heritage is the name his father adopted on arrival in America. It is not known just why, however, his father changed his name to the common Jewish surname of Isaacs from the rare but nondenominational Izac. After changing his name back to Izac in 1925, Edouard said, "It will even seem strange to me for a while. But it is my own name and I am the lineal descendent of a long line of Michel Izacs, so it is almost a duty to have the name preserved."

There is a possibility that there were Jews on Izacs's paternal side of the family. Without a doubt, however, Izac was a Roman Catholic and not a practicing Jew during his life and at his death.

★★★

27

Phillip C. Katz,
World War I, US Army

Company C, 363rd Infantry Regiment, 91st Infantry Division

Eclisfontaine, France, September 26, 1918

Date Presented: January 24, 1919

CITATION:

After his company had withdrawn for a distance of 200 yards on a line with the units on its flanks, Sgt. Katz learned that one of his comrades had been left wounded in an exposed position at the point from which the withdrawal had taken place. Voluntarily crossing an area swept by heavy machine gun fire, he advanced to where the wounded soldier lay and carried him to a place of safety.

PHILLIP (often misspelled as Philip) KATZ saved the life of a fellow soldier in the midst of bullet-swept "no man's land" in France and survived to spend the rest of his life in public service. Born on December 12, 1887, in San Francisco, Katz experienced the 1906 earthquake. His grandfather had come to California during the gold rush of 1849. Katz's father died when he was still a child, and he and a brother and sister were raised by his mother, Virginia Sylvia Barker Katz. Phillip grew up in the family home at 71 Parker Avenue and attended Hancock Grammar School and Polytechnic High School.

After high school, Katz wanted to join the navy and "see the world." His mother, needing his help with the family, convinced him to stay home where he worked as a butcher, in construction, and for the local gas company. Shortly after the United States entered World War I, the newly formed Selective Service System overruled Katz's mother's desire to keep him home and drafted him into the army.

Katz reported to Fort Lewis, Washington, where he received infantry training and joined Company C, 363rd Infantry Regiment, 91st Infantry Division, known as the "Wild West Division" because its ranks came from the far western states. The 91st Division sailed for France in July 1918. Held in reserve during the St. Mihiel Offensive, the 91st joined the front lines in the massive Meuse-Argonne battle in September.

On September 26, Company C, advancing against German positions near Eclisfontaine, France, encountered heavy machine-gun fire that drove the unit back. In a 1984 interview with the *San Francisco Chronicle*, Katz recalled, "We had withdrawn 200 yards and were straightening out the line with the units on our flanks. Someone told me that a friend of mine, Paul Page, had been left wounded. I stripped off everything but my gas mask and told the lieutenant I was going after him."

Katz dashed into "no man's land" amid heavy machine-gun and rifle fire. Ignoring the bullets striking all around him, he hoisted Page to his shoulders and hurried back to friendly lines. Katz later remembered, "That 200 yards was more like two miles. Page was a little runt. Short, but he was built out of brick. Felt like two tons."

When he got back to friendly lines, Katz was asked why he had taken such a risk. He replied, "Page would have done the same for me."

Page survived his wounds, and Katz returned to his infantryman duties as Company C helped push the Germans east across the Escaut River in the Battle of the Lys. The day before the Armistice, the army promoted Katz to sergeant.

When the war ended, the 91st remained in France near its border with Belgium. Gen. John De Goutte, commander of the Sixth French Army, under which the 91st served in the final days of the war, issued an order that stated in part, "I have found the same spirit of duty and discipline freely given in the 37th and 91st Divisions, United States Army, which brings about valiant soldiers and victorious armies. Glory to such troops and to such commanders. They have bravely contributed to the liberation of a part of Belgian territory and to final victory. The great nation to which they belong can be proud of them."

On January 24, 1919, at the 91st Division's headquarters, Gen. John J. Pershing, commander of the American Expeditionary Forces, presented Katz the

Medal of Honor. The 91st Division sailed for home in the spring of 1919 and demobilized at various camps in California, Washington, and Wyoming on May 14.

Katz, the only Californian to receive the Medal of Honor in World War I, returned to San Francisco to a thunderous welcome after his discharge. The *San Francisco Chronicle* headline declared him "California's Greatest Hero." After a month of vacation, Katz went to work as a bookkeeper for a navigation and coal company. An article in *The American Legion Weekly* on July 30, 1920, reported that Katz was like most other Medal of Honor recipients: "Living quietly, working hard, getting their share of the joys of life, and undergoing some of its trials, they are indistinguishable from the rest of us."

Asked in the article what it was like to return to civilian life, Katz said, "I found it hard at first to be confined to an office. I was restless, and for a month or two found it tough sitting still at a desk. The greatest change was getting back into bed sheets at night and eating three home-cooked meals a day. You can write a big capital 'NO!' as my answer to the question, 'Am I ever going back to France?'"

In 1923, Katz ran for, and was elected to, the San Francisco Board of Supervisors. In that position he authored resolutions to reduce the city's water and power rates to relieve the burden on the taxpayers by "cutting down a budget of ever-mounting millions." Two years later the citizens of San Francisco elected Katz as their public administrator. Over the following years, he settled thousands of estates when the deceased left no will. Katz remained the public administrator until his retirement on January 1, 1953.

Katz was a member of San Francisco's American Legion Post No. 1 and for a time served as the organization's president. He also was a 32nd Degree Scottish Rite Mason as a member of Argonne Lodge No. 514. In 1983 the State of California presented him a special state automobile license plate honoring Medal of Honor recipients.

An article in the January 8, 1984, edition of the *San Francisco Progress* reported that Katz had just turned ninety-six and that, although he had lost 60 percent of his sight, he still had a sense of humor, swam regularly at the Olympic Club, and liked to fish and travel. The piece added that Katz "is exactly the height and weight, 5-8 and 150, as the day General Pershing personally decorated him with the Congressional Medal of Honor. He has never married and has lived in the same house on Parker Avenue since his youth."

The article continued, "The modest Katz seldom attends public functions—he doesn't drink or smoke—but has never tired of travel. Despite his age, the nonagenarian is eagerly awaiting a Caribbean cruise in March."

Katz died on October 29, 1987, in French Hospital a few blocks from his Parker Avenue home just days before he was scheduled to act as the grand Marshal of the San Francisco Veterans Day Parade on November 11. A black-draped jeep took his place in the march.

Katz was the oldest Medal of Honor recipient at the time of his death. He is buried in Cypress Lawn Memorial Park (Section C) in Colma, California. He was survived by a niece, Philis Gold, and a nephew, Kenneth Ludlum.

Although Katz appears on many lists of Jewish Medal of Honor recipients, the Congressional Medal of Honor Society does not recognize him as such. There is no record of his religious beliefs. Neither his civilian nor military headstone contains a religious symbol. Neither do those of his siblings. Katz is a common name of both Jewish and German origin. At best, Katz can only be considered as possibly coming from Jewish lineage.

★★★

28

John Otto Siegel,
World War I, US Navy

USS *Mohawk*

Norfolk Naval Shipyard, Virginia, November 1, 1918

Date Presented: March 9, 1919

CITATION:

For extraordinary heroism while serving on board the Mohawk in performing a rescue mission aboard the schooner Hjeltenaes which was in flames on 1 November 1918. Going aboard the blazing vessel, Siegel rescued 2 men from the crew's quarters and went back the third time. Immediately after he had entered the crew's quarters, a steam pipe over the door bursted, making it impossible for him to escape. Siegel was overcome with smoke and fell to the deck, being finally rescued by some of the crew of the Mohawk who carried him out and rendered first aid.

JOHN SIEGEL left the US Navy with a Medal of Honor and a dishonorable discharge. His valor is beyond question; yet he serves as an example illustrating that brave sailors are not necessarily good sailors.

Much of the information about Siegel's youth is unavailable, and what is in the records is inconsistent from account to account. While all known documents agree to his April 21 birthday, the year varies from 1890 to 1891 and 1892. His possible birthplaces include Germany; Berlin, Wisconsin; Berlin, New York; or Milwaukee, Wisconsin. The most likely is Germany because the Canadian census of 1901 has him living with his parents, Julius N. and Annie Vance Siegel, in Winnipeg, Manitoba, after their arrival in 1899. The census notes that all three were born in Germany, they were Roman Catholic, and

Julius was employed as an architect. Siegel later claimed in enlistment papers to have been born in Wisconsin, likely to prevent any problem with not being a citizen. None of the papers confirm Siegel's later claim of being adopted.

By 1905, according to the Wisconsin census, the Siegels resided in Milwaukee with Julius still working as an architect. Nothing further is known about John until he enlisted in the US Navy for four years at the Milwaukee recruiting office on May 21, 1909. Siegel's enlistment form noted that he was living with his parents at 1307 Chestnut in Milwaukee, that he had been born on April 21, 1891, and that he was a citizen of the United States. It said that Siegel stood five feet six inches tall, weighed 123 pounds, and had blue-gray eyes, light brown hair, a ruddy complexion, scars on his right knee and back, and an atrophied right testis.

Ordinary Seaman Siegel reported to the USS *Constellation*, built in 1854 and the last sail-only warship designed and built by the US Navy. When he went aboard the veteran *Constellation* in Newport News, Virginia, it had been converted to a stationary training ship. Only four months after his enlistment, on September 21, Siegel's mother wrote to the secretary of the navy asking for her son to be discharged so he could return home and take care of his ailing parents. She concluded her letter by writing, "Hoping that you will not refuse the only wish of his poor father and mother."

The navy had no sympathy and denied the request. Siegel completed his training on December 23, 1909, and reported to the USS *Hancock*, a receiving ship docked in the New York Navy Yard, for further training and to await orders for assignment.

Three months later, on March 31, Siegel joined the crew of the battleship USS *Virginia*, docked for modifications at Hampton Roads, Virginia. While assigned to the *Virginia*, Siegel spent twenty-five days in the Norfolk Naval Hospital being treated for "dementia." From what little remains of his medical records, it appears that Siegel mostly suffered from depression.

On December 31, Siegel transferred to the USS *Franklin*, a screw frigate serving as a receiving ship at the Norfolk Naval Station. While aboard the *Franklin*, Siegel received punishments of extra duty and fines for being absent without leave for seven days, shirking of orders, disrespecting his superiors, and not taking proper care of his gear. As a result of these actions, plus his medical issues, he was not assigned to a regular ship until June 30, 1911, when he joined the USS *North Dakota*, an Atlantic Fleet vessel that frequently docked in New York City.

Siegel evidently performed adequately aboard the *North Dakota* because on October 1, 1911, the navy promoted him from ordinary seaman to seaman. When the *North Dakota* next put into harbor in New York, Siegel met Teresa Rose Neilas, daughter of John and Margaret Buckley Neilas. On September 22, 1912, the two married in St. James Catholic Church in Newark, New Jersey, and took up residence in the city at 156 Green Street. Apparently, Siegel much preferred married life to that of a sailor and did not return to his ship when his leave expired on September 25.

The navy listed him as a deserter but took no real action to apprehend him for more than two years. This was because deserters often returned of their own volition or were arrested on other charges and turned over to naval control. When neither of these occurred, the navy issued a reward notice of $25 for his apprehension on January 25, 1915. The notice included his and his wife's last known address on Green Street. A week later a New York City detective apprehended Siegel and turned him over to the navy on February 6.

Siegel faced a general court martial for his absence of two years and four months. The court found him guilty and sentenced him to hard labor for one and a half years with a dishonorable discharged upon completion of his sentence. Siegel had to forfeit all pay except for $3 a month for necessary prison expenses and $20 at his release. A review by the judge advocate general of the Department of the Navy on March 5, 1915, approved the sentence—except he reduced the confinement to one year.

After his trial, the navy transferred Siegel to the prison ship the USS *Southery*, docked in the harbor of Portsmouth, New Hampshire. He behaved so well that the prison released Siegel on October 27, 1915, after only eight months. The prison commander wrote in the discharge papers, "During this time his conduct was excellent, and he is recommended for reenlistment in the service."

After his discharge, Siegel returned with his wife to Milwaukee, where he worked as a chauffeur for the Wells Fargo Company. There he and Teresa had their first and only child, Margaret Jean. Siegel continued his efforts to reenlist in the navy but was turned down until the navy needed more sailors with the outbreak of World War I. On December 15, 1917, the naval recruiting officer in Milwaukee swore in Siegel for a four-year tour. The 1917 enlistment papers recorded his birth year as 1890 and showed that he had gained twenty pounds, to 144, and added a tattoo of a shield, anchor, and "USN."

Assigned to the Norfolk Navy Yard, Siegel performed a multitude of duties aboard ships and on shore. He performed well enough to be promoted to coxswain on June 1, 1918, and to boatswain's mate 2nd class on September 1. On November 1, 1918, Siegel was aboard the tugboat USS *Mohawk* as it operated in and around the Norfolk Navy Yard, serving the fleet by towing barges and aiding naval vessels. As the tugboat neared the Belt Line Railroad bridge in Norfolk harbor, the crew saw that the wooden civilian schooner *Hjeltenaes* was on fire as it sat tied up along the structure. The tug maneuvered near the schooner, and Siegel went aboard, where he rescued a man overcome by smoke in the crew quarters. He went back and saved a second man before he attempted his third trip into the burning vessel. He was so overcome by smoke and heat himself that when his crewmates rushed him to the hospital, doctors initially feared he would not live.

However, he did recover and returned to duty at the Norfolk Navy Yard. On March 9, 1919, the navy awarded him the Medal of Honor. Siegel's medal was the Tiffany Cross, a design by the Tiffany Company that the navy adopted in 1917 and awarded to only twenty-one sailors and seven marines before returning to the five-pointed star design in 1942.

On March 31, 1919, Siegel transferred to the newly commissioned USS *Hopewell,* a destroyer based at Norfolk. Siegel must not have liked life aboard a destroyer because less than three months later, on June 16, he once again deserted. The navy issued a reward notice for his apprehension on August 27, and he was soon in custody and facing another general court martial. Prior to his trial, Siegel underwent a psychiatric evaluation.

The senior medical officer for Naval Base Norfolk issued the findings of the evaluation on September 22, 1919. He included the report from the director of the Base Psychiatric Division that stated, "This man was injured in a fire in 1918 when he rescued some men from a burning ship. For this he was awarded a Congressional Medal of Honor. However he claims to have worried and been exceedingly nervous for several months subsequent to this event. Has recently been worrying very much over domestic affairs. He appears somewhat depressed and seems to think that things have 'gone wrong' with him all his life. States that he found out only a short time ago that he was an adopted child and this has preyed on his mind to some extent."

These factors apparently had little influence on the senior medical officer's findings. He concluded, "In concurrence with the above report, the Senior Medical Officer is of the opinion that this man may be considered responsible for his acts."

On October 27, 1919, the judge advocate general of the Department of the Navy issued the results of Siegel's court martial. It stated, "The above named man who was recently tried by general court martial at the Naval Operation Base, at Hampton Roads, Va., was found guilty of 'absence from station and duty after leave had expired,' and sentenced to be reduced to seaman and to be confined for a period of six (6) months, then to be dishonorably discharged from the United States naval service and to suffer all other accessories of said sentence, as prescribed by the 'Naval Courts and Boards' Sec. 349."

The report continued, saying that the Department of the Navy approved the sentence. However, because of mitigating circumstances (likely Sigel being a Medal of Honor recipient), the confinement was changed from the brig to restriction aboard ship or station. It further stated that if Siegel conducted himself properly for six months, the dishonorable discharge would be waived and he would be allowed to remain in the navy. It he did not behave, his commanding officer had the right to execute the dishonorable discharge at any time.

Siegel failed to take advantage of the offered opportunity. On March 15, 1920, his commanding officer ordered him to be dishonorably discharged. Siegel would later claim that the action was taken because he was "one day over leave." Other evidence indicates the discharge was the result of Siegel's attempt to obtain money "under false pretenses."

Whatever the reason, Siegel was again a civilian. He returned to New York City, where he resumed work as a chauffeur and later became an ironworker on the city's bridges. However, he again began lobbying to return to the navy. On October 20, 1920, he wrote a letter to the Department of the Navy through the Newark, New Jersey, recruiting station, asking to be reinstated. He concluded by saying that he had committed himself to serve "Honestly and faithfully." The navy denied his request.

Siegel, writing on stationary from the Delaware Hotel in Milwaukee where he resided, again wrote the Navy Department on May 23, 1929, requesting permission to reenlist. The navy responded promptly in its letter of June 13: "Replying to your letter of recent date, you are advised that your re-enlistment in the Navy is not authorized inasmuch as only men who have been discharged with Good or Honorable discharges are being accepted for re-enlistment."

Apparently, Siegel had abandoned his wife and daughter sometime earlier. On September 30, 1918, Teresa wrote the Navy Department to say that she had not heard from her husband since the previous July and not received her allotment for August. She added, " . . . it has occurred to me that he may have deserted the navy."

There is no record of Siegel ever seeing his wife and daughter after his dismissal from the service. In about 1930, Siegel left the East Coast for Oklahoma, where he went to work in the oil fields. Although still legally married to Teresa, he met and married a woman named Mary Lou in Henryetta. From Oklahoma, Siegel traveled west in the early 1930s and found employment as an ironworker in the construction of Boulder Dam on the Colorado River between Nevada and Arizona.

On May 28, 1935, the director of claims services for the New York chapter of the American Red Cross wrote the Navy Department on Siegel's behalf. The letter stated that all his belongings, including his Medal of Honor, had been destroyed in a fire that had swept through the workers' quarters at the Boulder Dam project and asked how a replacement medal could be procured. The navy responded on June 17, and Siegel received a replacement medal.

Writing from the New York City YMCA on November 26, 1936, Siegel once again asked the Navy Department to be allowed to enlist for the third time. The navy denied his request. According to 1940 census records, Siegel resided in Baltimore, Maryland, but in April 1941 he wrote from San Antonio, Texas, to the navy asking for a second replacement of his Medal of Honor, which had been destroyed in another home fire. On July 31, 1941, the Navy Department responded by denying his request because of his dishonorable discharge, adding that his earlier replacement had been sent contrary to current regulations. There was conjecture that Siegel might have sold one or both medals and that they had not been destroyed in fires.

Despite his earlier service and discharges, Siegel had to fill out a World War II draft registration card. He registered as John Robert Siegel, born in Berlin, New York, and living in the Hotel London in Janesville, Wisconsin. On various other documents during this period, he also used the name Jack Atto Siegel.

Siegel died of lung cancer on August 15, 1943, in Gary, Indiana. His death certificate shows Jonon O. Siegel as having lived at 848 Maryland Street in Gary with his wife Mary Lou. It is not known if "Jonon" was a typographical error (possibly instead of "Jno.," an abbreviation for John) or another alias. Siegel is buried in Gary's Mount Mercy Cemetery (Section 12A, Row 5, Grave 11).

The courage of John Siegel, at least at one time on one date, cannot be questioned. Because of his parents' age, it is likely that he was adopted and that the adoption occurred before they departed Germany for Canada. His being adopted as a very young child also makes sense with his later claim of not knowing that he was not the natural child of the Siegels. Other than his name appearing on many lists of Jewish Medal of Honor recipients, there is no evidence of his being a Jew other than his adoptive parents' name. His headstone bears a Christian cross. There is, of course, the possibility that he was born Jewish before his adoption, but there is no surviving evidence as to validate of this theory. The Congressional Medal of Honor Society does not include Siegel as a Jewish recipient.

★★★

29

Anthony Michael Stein,
World War II, US Marine Corps

Company A, 1st Battalion, 28th Marines, 5th US Marine Division

Iwo Jima, February 19, 1945

Date Presented: February 19, 1946

CITATION:

For conspicuous gallantry and intrepidity at the risk of his life above and beyond the call of duty while serving with Company A, 1st Battalion, 28th Marines, 5th Marine Division, in action against enemy Japanese forces on Iwo Jima, in the Volcano Islands, 19 February 1945. The first man of his unit to be on station after hitting the beach in the initial assault, Cpl. Stein, armed with a personally improvised aircraft-type weapon, provided rapid covering fire as the remainder of his platoon attempted to move into position. When his comrades were stalled by a concentrated machinegun and mortar barrage, he gallantly stood upright and exposed himself to the enemy's view, thereby drawing the hostile fire to his own person and enabling him to observe the location of the furiously blazing hostile guns. Determined to neutralize the strategically placed weapons, he boldly charged the enemy pillboxes 1 by 1 and succeeded in killing 20 of the enemy during the furious single-handed assault. Cool and courageous under the merciless hail of exploding shells and bullets which fell on all sides, he continued to deliver the fire of his skillfully improvised weapon at a tremendous rate of speed which rapidly exhausted his ammunition. Undaunted, he removed his helmet and shoes to expedite his movements and ran back to the beach for additional ammunition, making a total of 8 trips under intense fire and carrying or assisting a wounded man back each time. Despite the unrelenting savagery and confusion of battle, he rendered prompt assistance to his platoon whenever the unit was in position, directing the fire of a half-track against a stubborn pillbox until he had effected the ultimate destruction of the Japanese fortification. Later in the day, although his weapon was twice shot from his hands, he personally covered the withdrawal of his platoon to the company position. Stouthearted and indomitable, Cpl. Stein, by his aggressive initiative sound judgment, and unwavering devotion to duty in the face of terrific odds, contributed materially to the fulfillment of his mission, and his outstanding valor throughout the bitter hours of conflict sustains and enhances the highest traditions of the U. S. Naval Service.

ANTHONY MICHAEL "Tony" Stein used the skills he learned as a civilian tool and die maker to improvise an aircraft machine gun into the personal weapon he used to earn the Medal of Honor during the initial assault on the island of Iwo Jima. Tony's parents, the German-speaking Steven and Rose Stein, immigrated to the United States early in the twentieth century from Yugoslavia. Born on September 30, 1921, in Dayton, Ohio, Tony attended the city's public schools before dropping out of Kiser High School his freshman year.

After a series of menial odd jobs, he found employment in a machine shop at Dayton's Patterson Field. He then did a tour with the Civilian Conversation Corps, working construction and in a lumber camp. Tony then returned to Dayton and became a tool and die apprentice in the local Delco Products plant. In 1940 he saved the life of a boy drowning in the Mad River. In February of 1942, Stein—standing five feet six inches tall and weighing 128 pounds—won his division in the Dayton Golden Glove Championship.

With his job at Delco considered essential, Stein was deferred from the draft. He, however, volunteered for the Marine Corps in September 1942. Upon completion of boot camp, he attended jump school and joined the elite Paramarines of the 1st Parachute Regiment of the 3rd Marine Division. Stein fought with the regiment in the Vella Lavella and Bougainville Campaigns. He became particularly adept in countering Japanese snipers, killing five in a single day.

After the Battle of Bougainville, when the Marine Corps disbanded the Paramarines, Stein and his fellow paratroopers returned to the States to assist in forming the 5th Marine Division at Camp Pendleton, California. While on leave, he married Joan Stominger, whom he had met while working at Patterson Field before the war.

No longer was he the slight boy who had fought in the Golden Glove competition; the Stein who returned to the Pacific Theater with the 5th Marines had grown two inches in height and now weighed a muscular 190 pounds. Stein acquired a Browning .30-caliber machine gun from a crashed aircraft. Using his prewar tool and die skills, he modified the machine gun, which he called the "Stinger," by adding an M-1 Garand buttstock, a BAR rear sight and bipod, and a fabricated trigger. He then had a weapon that could fire 500 rounds per minute.

Stein and his fellow marines went ashore on Iwo Jima on February 19, 1944. Charging forward, Stein used his modified machine gun to neutralize Japanese pillboxes. When he expended the ammunition of his rapid-firing weapon, he picked up a wounded marine and returned to the beach for more rounds. By day's end, he had made eight trips back to the beach for additional ammo and to deliver fallen comrades to medical assistance. For these actions he was recommended for the Medal of Honor.

The 28th Regiment and Stein pushed on into the island's interior and captured Mount Suribachi, where the famous flag-raising took place on February 23. Stein was wounded in the advance up the mountain and was evacuated to a hospital ship. After a brief stay he returned to his unit and on March 1 was killed by a sniper while leading a reconnaissance patrol. He was buried in the 5th Division Cemetery on the island.

On February 19, 1946, a year after his heroic actions with his "Stinger" on Iwo Jima, Adm. Richard Pennoyer presented Stein's Medal of Honor to his widow at the Ohio capitol. Stein's remains were returned to Ohio for reinterment on December 17, 1948, in Dayton's Cavalry Cemetery following funeral services at Our Lady of Rosary Church.

There are claims in several books about the Battle of Iwo Jima that Stein identified as Jewish. The only corroboration for that claim is a single page of death notifications in the files of the National Jewish Welfare Board's Bureau of War Records. There is far more support for his being a practicing Catholic. The baptismal register of Our Lady of Rosary in Dayton, where Stein's funeral was held, records that he was baptized there on October 9, 1921, ten days after his birth. A copy of a letter to his wife in the files of the Congressional of Medal of Honor Society from the chaplain of Stein's marine unit states that he was "conspicuous" in being a Catholic. It is also noteworthy that several of Stein's fellow marines reported that he had a large black panther tattooed on his left arm—a practice not approved by practicing Jews.

For these reasons the Medal of Honor Society does not include Stein as a Jew or even as possibly being Jewish. However, because of the chance that one or both of his parents were of Jewish ancestry and the document in the National Jewish Welfare Board files, he is included in this study as possibly being a Jew.

PART 4

Medal of Honor Recipients
Incorrectly Identified as Jewish

30

Donald K. Schwab,
World War II, US Army

Company E, 15th Infantry Regiment, 3d Infantry Division

Lure, France, September 17, 1944

Date Presented: March 18, 2014

CITATION:

First Lieutenant Donald K. Schwab distinguished himself by acts of gallantry and intrepidity above and beyond the call of duty while serving as the Commander of Company E, 15th Infantry Regiment, 3d Infantry Division, during combat operations against an armed enemy near Lure, France on September 17, 1944. That afternoon, as First Lieutenant Schwab led his company across four hundred yards of exposed ground, an intense, grazing burst of machinegun and machine pistol fire sprung forth without warning from a fringe of woods directly in front of the American force. First Lieutenant Schwab quickly extricated his men from the attempted ambush and led them back to a defiladed position. Soon after, he was ordered to overwhelm the enemy line. He rapidly organized his men into a skirmish line and, with indomitable courage, again led them forward into the lethal enemy fire. When halted a second time, First Lieutenant Schwab moved from man to man to supervise collection of the wounded and organize his company's withdrawal. From defilade, he rallied his decimated force for a third charge on the hostile strong point and successfully worked his way to within fifty yards of the Germans before ordering his men to hit the dirt. While automatic weapons fire blazed around him, he rushed forward alone, firing his carbine at the German foxholes, aiming for the vital enemy machine-pistol nest which had sparked the German resistance and caused heavy casualties among his men. Silhouetted through the mist and rain by enemy flares, he charged to the German emplacement, ripped the half-cover off the hostile firing pit, struck the German gunner on the head with his carbine butt and dragged the German back through a hail of fire to friendly lines. First Lieutenant Schwab's action so disorganized hostile infantry resistance that the enemy forces withdrew, abandoning their formidable defensive line.

DONALD SCHWAB joined the army right out of high school and advanced in rank to 1st lieutenant in command of an infantry company in World War II. After the war, he returned to his rural Nebraska home and lived to be eighty-six years old before his death in 2005. Nine years later the Medal of Honor for his valor that he earned on the battlefield was finally awarded.

Born on December 6, 1918, in Hooper, Nebraska, to parents Harry J. and Catherine Schwein Schwab, Donald attended District 15 Elementary School and graduated from Hooper High School in 1936. Schwab would later recall that, in the late 1930s, he and many others in Hooper realized that there was going to be a war in Europe in a few years. Sharing the great patriotic spirit of his neighbors, he was happy to sign up for the draft in the fall of 1940. Scheduled to be inducted in March of 1941, he did not enter the US Army as an infantry private until June 16, 1942, because there were so many volunteers standing in line.

Schwab trained at Fort Leonard Wood, Missouri, and Camp Breckenridge, Kentucky. By the time he joined the 15th Infantry Regiment of the 3rd Infantry Division, he had attended Officers Candidate School and become a 2nd lieutenant. The 3rd Infantry Division would fight the Axis on all five fronts of the European Theater. They deployed from Camp Pickett, Virginia, on October 24, 1942, and went ashore at Fedala in North Africa as a part of Operation Torch. From there, the 3rd's troops captured much of French Morocco.

Leaving Africa, the 15th Regiment made an amphibious assault on the Italian island of Sicily in July 1943 and then advanced to Salerno in September. Schwab fought in the regiment's Company E while fellow infantryman Audie Murphy in Company B became the war's most decorated soldier. Schwab suffered a wound to his knee in a fight near the Volturno River. When he left the hospital in January 1944, he rejoined Company E at Anzio where, he later recalled, they "lived like a bunch of rats" in foxholes. A second wound, this time to his shoulder, returned Schwab to the hospital. On his release, he rejoined his company in Rome and then participated in the 3rd Division's invasion of southern France on the Rivera in August.

Schwab, although only a 1st lieutenant, commanded Company E in its attack across France. On September 17, 1944, near Lure, a German machine-gun position held up Company E's advance. Schwab went to the front and led his company across 400 yards of open ground toward the enemy. Forced back three times, Schwab charged forward alone over the final 50 yards. When he reached the German machine gun, he fired into the bunker and then ripped its protective overhead cover away. He then struck the primary machine gunner over the head with his carbine and dragged him back to friendly lines. Schwab's attack so disorganized the enemy troops that they abandoned their defenses and retreated. Many years later he told his son, Terry, that he hit that German so hard that "if he was still alive today he'd still have a lump on his head."

About the battle, Schwab later recalled, his company had only thirty-two men. He said, "I was the only officer among the 32. There was a fire fight, I remember grabbing a machinegunner. I hit him over the head and knocked him out. I didn't want to kill him."

Schwab received the Distinguished Service Cross for his actions. On November 2, Company E attacked the German-held town of St. Die, France. Schwab described once again being under machine-gun fire and earning his third Purple Heart, saying, "The Germans missed the first time but then shot me in the right arm with the next volley. That was it. The injury sent me back to the States in December of 1944 and I missed the Battle of the Bulge."

After recovering from his wound, Schwab remained on Stateside duty until his discharge on October 26, 1945. He immediately returned home to Nebraska, where he later said, "I made up my mind when I was over in Europe during World War II that if I ever got out of there alive, I'd return home and that they'd never get me out of Hooper."

Virgil, Schwab's brother, was not so fortunate. Capt. Virgil Schwab, a graduate of the US Military Academy at West Point, went missing in action when his bomber went down in the South Pacific in July 1942. His remains were never recovered.

Schwab married Maralee Janssen in Hooper's Grace Lutheran Church on September 18, 1946, and over the years they had three daughters and two sons. He farmed for a few years before becoming a rural mail carrier for the US Postal Service in 1951, which is where he worked until his retirement in 1980. Schwab was an active member of Hooper's American Legion Post 18 and Hooper-Winslow Veterans of Foreign Wars Post 10535. In retirement, he liked to garden and play golf. For nearly sixty years, he commanded the firing squad for military funerals and Memorial Day observances.

An article in Nebraska's *Oakland Independent* in 1995 quoted Schwab about why he rarely mentioned the war. He said, "When you go through so many artillery attacks and hear so many shots and so many cries, you get a little silly. It was just easier not talking about it."

Schwab died on February 19, 2005, in Omaha at the University of Nebraska Medical Center. His services were held in Grace Lutheran Church and he is buried in the Hooper Cemetery (Section 7, Lot 4, Grave 3). People in Hooper remember Schwab as a friendly man to whom they liked to talk. His family described him as a humble person and a great husband, father, and grandfather.

Nine years after his death, Department of Defense officials announced the upgrade of twenty-four Distinguished Service Crosses to Medals of Honor after a lengthy review of records. Most recipients were minorities. The military officials stated that, while the ethnicity or religious affiliation of some upgrades was uncertain, their battlefield actions were found to deserve the highest honor. On March 18, 2014, Pres. Barack Obama presented the medals in a White House ceremony. Terry, Schwab's son, accept the Medal of Honor in his behalf.

Sen. Deb Fischer (R-NE) issued the following statement about the service and sacrifice of Schwab:

> We all owe a tremendous debt of gratitude to First Lieutenant Donald Schwab for his heroic acts of service during World War II. Schwab demonstrated uncommon valor on the battlefield in Lure, France, as he bravely led his men into combat before charging the enemy alone, forcing the Germans to retreat. I join the president, Nebraskans, and all Americans in thanking First Lieutenant Schwab and each Medal of Honor recipient for their extraordinary service on behalf of our country. We honor these great Americans and all our nation's heroes who fight dutifully to protect and defend our freedom.

Maralee Schwab was not able to attend the ceremony because of declining health, but she did watch via a live stream to her care center. She was, however, able to attend an honor ceremony for her husband at the Nebraska State Capitol on June 7, 2014. An article in the *Lincoln Journal Star* said, "She touched the framed flag gently, her hands trembling as the flashes of cameras reflected off the marble tile of the 14th floor of the State Capitol. The click of the shutters captured the moment: the 92-year-old widow accepting the Medal of Honor for her late husband, 1st Lt. Donald K. Schwab."

Although the Department of Defense made it clear in its announcement of the twenty-four Medals of Honor that some of the recipients were not minorities by race or religion, most of the national media included Schwab in the list of Jewish recipients. As a result, his name appears today on many lists of Jewish Americans who have received the medal. There is no evidence that Schwab was a Jew. The Congressional Medal of Honor Society does not include him on its list of Jewish Americans. His obituary states that he was a member the Redeemer Lutheran Church in Hooper, that he served on the church council for many years, and that he acted as treasurer for the building fund of a new church building. His headstone has a Latin cross.

Schwab was not a Jew. He is included in this section to clarify why he should not be included as a Jewish recipient.

★★★

31

William F. Leonard,
World War II, US Army

Company C, 30th Infantry Regiment, 3rd Infantry Division

St. Die, France, November 7, 1944

Date Presented: March 18, 2014

CITATION:

Private First Class William F. Leonard distinguished himself by acts of gallantry and intrepidity above and beyond the call of duty while serving as a Squad Leader in Company C, 30th Infantry Regiment, 3d Infantry Division during combat operations against an armed enemy near St. Die, France on November 7, 1944. Private First Class Leonard's platoon was reduced to eight men as a result of blistering artillery, mortar, machinegun, and rifle fire. Private First Class Leonard led the survivors in an assault over a hill covered by trees and shrubs which the enemy continuously swept with automatic weapons fire. Ignoring bullets which pierced his pack, Private First Class Leonard killed two snipers at ranges of fifty and seventy-five yards and engaged and destroyed a machinegun nest with grenades, killing its two-man crew. Though momentarily stunned by an exploding bazooka shell, Private First Class Leonard relentlessly advanced, ultimately knocking out a second machinegun nest and capturing the roadblock objective.

WILLIAM LEONARD fought across Italy, in France, and into Germany as he participated in three beach assault landings and earned the Distinguished Service Cross. Born on August 9, 1913, in the "Irish section" of Lockport, New York, to William and Mary Male Leonard, he finished high school and then moved to Portland, Maine, where he enjoyed playing baseball while he worked as sales clerk and a butcher.

Drafted as an infantryman on November 17, 1942, Leonard joined the 3rd Infantry Division in time to participate in the amphibious landing at Licata, Italy, in the battle for the island of Sicily in July 1943. The 3rd Division then invaded mainland Italy at Salerno in September and attacked up the Italian "boot" to Monte Cassino. Leonard made his second amphibious landing at Anzio and then pushed on with his unit to capture Rome. On August 15, 1944, Leonard made his third amphibious landing at St. Tropez in the invasion of southern France. The 3rd Division then advanced up the Rhone Valley, through the Vosges Mountains, and to Strasbourg on the Rhine River in late November. This operation helped clear the Colmar Pocket in January 1945 and in March penetrated the Siegfried Line to cross into Germany. In the final month of fighting, the 3rd Division captured Nuremberg and Augsburg and was near Salzburg when the war ended.

Leonard advanced in rank from private to staff sergeant as his regiment advanced across Europe. On November 7, 1944, Leonard's regiment fought to push the Germans out of northeastern France near St. Die. The Germans countered with mortar, artillery, and machine-gun fire that reduced Leonard's platoon to eight men. Leonard took charge of the survivors and moved forward toward an enemy roadblock. Although wounded, Leonard killed two snipers and neutralized two German machine-gun positions before capturing the objective.

The New York infantryman received the Distinguished Service Cross for the action. Other than the medal, his reward was to continue the offensive on into Germany. By the end of the war he had earned, in addition to the DSC, the Combat Infantryman Badge, a Bronze Star, a Purple Heart, and a Good Conduct Medal.

Leonard returned to Lockhart after his discharge on November 7, 1945, married Mary Barone, and had three daughters. He worked at Harrison Radiator Division of the General Motors Corporation. It was close enough to his home that he could walk to work daily, despite a lingering limp from his war wounds. Every Christmas, Leonard came home in a taxi filled with toys and other presents, although his wife had already done the family's Christmas shopping.

He rarely talked about the war, and few were aware of his great bravery in capturing a German roadblock. His daughters later recalled that their father was a quiet, hardworking man who had a deep sense of patriotism and a dry sense of humor. His only acknowledgment of his military service was his army uniform, which he kept hanging in his garage. The only stories they remember his telling about the war was receiving Communion in a bomb-damaged church in Strasbourg and finding some of the best-tasting bread he had ever eaten in an abandoned French bakery. He was a member of the Veterans of Foreign Wars Post 2535.

Leonard died at age seventy-one in the Lockport Memorial Hospital on August 4, 1985. He is buried in Lockport's Cold Spring Cemetery (Section 7, Lot 64, Grave 4).

In 2014 the congressionally mandated review of minority recipients of the DSC to see if any had been denied the Medal of Honor because of racism were released. Leonard was one of the twenty-four recommended for an upgrade of his DSC to the Medal of Honor. On March, 18, 2014, Pres. Barack Obama awarded Leonard's Medal of Honor to his eldest daughter, Patricia Kennedy, in a White House ceremony. President Obama said, "These veterans lived out their lives in the country they helped defend, doing what they loved, like William Leonard, who at age 71 passed away in his backyard, sitting in his chair, listening to his beloved Yankees play on the radio."

During the review, several service members were recommended for upgrades who were not African American, Asian American, Hispanic American, or Jewish American but were deserving of the award. Leonard was one of those, as there is no record or family remembrance of Leonard being Jewish. He was a Catholic, and his funeral services were held in Lockport at St. Mary's Catholic Church. The Congressional Medal of Honor Society does not include him or three others from the review on their Jewish recipient list. Since their names sounded somewhat Jewish, many in the press and across the country assumed they were Jews. Ironically, the Jewish community itself may have been guilty as well, as the four are included on many lists of Jewish recipients.

Shortly after the presentation of Leonard's Medal of Honor, the city of Lockport honored him and two other of their fellow citizens who had earned the award with a memorial. It stands at the intersection of Lake Avenue (New York State Route 78) and Old Niagara Road.

32

Alfred B. Nietzel,

World War II, US Army

Company H, 16th Infantry Regiment, 1st Infantry Division

Heistern, Germany, November 18, 1944

Date Presented: March 18, 2014

CITATION:

Sergeant Alfred B. Nietzel distinguished himself by acts of gallantry and intrepidity above and beyond the call of duty while serving as a section leader for Company H, 16th Infantry Regiment, 1st Infantry Division during combat operations against an armed enemy in Heistern, Germany on November 18, 1944. That afternoon, Sergeant Nietzel fought tenaciously to repel a vicious enemy attack against his unit. Sergeant Nietzel employed accurate, intense fire from his machinegun and successfully slowed the hostile advance. However, the overwhelming enemy force continued to press forward. Realizing he desperately needed reinforcements, Sergeant Nietzel ordered the three remaining members of his squad to return to the company command post and secure aid. He immediately turned his attention to covering their movement with his fire. After expending all his machinegun ammunition, Sergeant Nietzel began firing his rifle into the attacking ranks until he was killed by the explosion of an enemy grenade. Sergeant Nietzel's extraordinary heroism and selflessness at the cost of his own life above and beyond the call of duty, are in keeping with the highest traditions of military service and reflect great credit upon himself, his unit and the United States Army.

THE STORY OF Alfred Nietzel is brief. Still in his early twenties, he sacrificed his life while protecting his fellow soldiers and posthumously received the Medal of Honor for his bravery seventy years later. Born on April 27, 1921, in Fordham, Bronx, New York, to Albert C. and Ruth Lawrence Nietzel, Alfred did not remain long with his parents. His father was committed to the state mental institution in Rockland and then Orange Counties before Alfred's tenth birthday. The senior Nietzel remained institutionalized until his death in 1971.

According to the census, Alfred and his two brothers were living in a foster home in Harrison, New York, in the 1930s. Alfred dropped out of high school after two years and went to work as a machinist in Nassau County, Long Island. On October 15, 1940, he enlisted in the US Army as an infantryman at Nassau, New York. His enlistment papers note that he stood sixty-five inches tall, weighted 144 pounds, and was single without dependents.

Nietzel initially enlisted for duty in the "Panama Canal Department" but soon joined the 16th Infantry Regiment, part of the 1st Infantry Division (nicknamed "The Big Red One"), stationed at Fort Jay on Governor's Island. The City of New York and its mayor, Fiorello H. LaGuardia, so liked and respected the regiment that it became known as "New York's Own," and "The Sidewalks of New York" became the regimental marching song.

The 16th Infantry transferred to Fort Devens, Massachusetts, in February 1941 and then participated in the Carolina Maneuvers. In April 1942 the regiment sailed for England, where it trained before going ashore near Arzew, French Morocco, in the invasion of North Africa on November 8, 1942. Nietzel and the 1st Division helped capture Oran and then fought in the battles of the Ousseltia Valley, Kasserine Pass, El Guettar, and Mateur in Tunisia. For its performance at Kasserine Pass, the French government awarded the 16th Infantry the Croix de Guerre, and it received the Presidential Unit Citation from the US government for its performance at Mateur.

On July 10, 1943, the 16th Regiment made an amphibious assault on Sicily. Over the next three weeks, the soldiers faced bitter fighting with German infantry and panzer units before securing the Italian island. From Sicily, Nietzel and the 16th Regiment returned to England where, over the next seven months, they received replacements and trained for the Allied invasion of mainland Europe.

Early on the morning of June 6, 1944, the 16th Infantry made an amphibious assault on Omaha Beach at Normandy, France. They met strong resistance from the German defenders. With his men momentarily halted on the beach, Col. George A. Taylor, the regiment's commander, stood in the midst of fire and shouted to his troops, "The only men who remain on this beach are dead and those who are about to die! Let's get moving!" Move they did, and soon the regiment pushed inland.

The 16th Infantry Regiment pursued the Germans across France and destroyed much of their Seventh Army at the Falaise Gap. After another victory at Mons, Belgium, the 1st Infantry Division attacked toward Aachen, Germany. On September19, they began a three-month-long battle in the Hurtgen Forest along the Belgium-Germany border that produced some of the most intense and bloody fighting of the war.

Nietzel, by virtue of his leadership abilities and his survivability, advanced in rank to sergeant in charge of a squad in the 16th Regiment's offensive. On November 18, 1944, Nietzel's squad attempted to neutralize a German position on a hill near Heistern, Germany, when the enemy counterattacked. Outmanned and outgunned, Nietzel ordered his men to retreat while he took up a .30-caliber machine gun to cover their withdrawal. He fired until he ran out of ammunition for the machine gun and then picked up his rifle and continued the fight until he finally fell, mortally wounded by a German hand grenade.

The army posthumously awarded Nietzel the Distinguished Service Cross. Before his death, he had also earned a Bronze Star and the Combat Infantryman Badge. He was buried in the Henri-Chapelle American Cemetery and Memorial at Welkenraedt, Belgium. On April 19, 1949, his remains were repatriated to the United States and reinterred in Long Island National Cemetery (Section J, Grave 14185) in Farmingdale, New York. He lies next to his brother William E., who died of noncombat causes on April 6, 1944, while assigned to the US Army Air Corps in England. There was no known photograph of Nietzel until a distant family member discovered a picture of the hero in 2020.

Nietzel's valor remained mostly unknown or forgotten until the congressionally mandated review that concluded in 2014. On March 18, 2014, Pres. Barack Obama awarded the Medal of Honor to Nietzel in a White House ceremony. Accepting the medal on his cousin's behalf was Robert L. Nietzel of San Juan Capistrano, California. Although the Department of Defense announced that Nietzel and three others had their records reviewed as possible minorities, there was no evidence that Nietzel was Jewish. Most newspapers and other media did not carry that explanation and either alluded to, or directly stated, that Nietzel and the others were Jewish Americans. As a result,

Nietzel incorrectly appears on most lists of Jewish Medal of Honor recipients.

Nietzel's cousin Robert, a Korean War veteran of the 24th Infantry Division, said that he was nine years younger than Alfred and barely knew him. He stated that the Nietzels immigrated from Germany "several generations earlier" but that he had no knowledge of there being any Jews in the family background. The Congressional Medal of Honor Society concurs and does not list Nietzel as Jewish American.

Shortly after the medal presentation in Washington, DC, the 1st Infantry Division dedicated the Medal of Honor Room in the Cantigny Dining Facility at Fort Riley, Kansas, which contains the Medal of Honor citations of the unit's soldiers. Robert Nietzel attended the dedication and said, "It was very important for me to be here today and to be a part of it. My cousin is in that room on the wall and he will forever be a part of the 1st Infantry Division. People have no idea what a soldier goes through and this would be good for them. I think this should be something everyone gets a chance to see."

33

Jack Weinstein,
Korea, US Army

Company G, 2nd Battalion. 21st Infantry Regiment, 24th Infantry Division
Kumsong, Korea, October 19, 1951
Date Presented: March 18, 2014

CITATION:

Sergeant Jack Weinstein distinguished himself by acts of gallantry and intrepidity above and beyond the call of duty while leading 1st Platoon, Company G, 21st Infantry Regiment, 24th Infantry Division in Kumsong, Korea on October 19, 1951. That afternoon, thirty enemy troops counterattacked Sergeant Weinstein's platoon. Most of the platoon's members had been wounded in the previous action and withdrew under the heavy fire. Sergeant Weinstein, however, remained in his position and continued to fight off the onrushing enemy, killing at least six with his M-1 rifle before running out of ammunition. Although under extremely heavy enemy fire, Sergeant Weinstein refused to withdraw and continued fighting by throwing enemy hand grenades found lying near his position. He again halted the enemy's progress and inflicted numerous casualties. Alone and unaided, he held the ground which his platoon had fought tenaciously to take and held out against overwhelming odds until another platoon was able to relieve him and drive back the enemy. Sergeant Weinstein's leg had been broken by an enemy grenade and old wounds suffered in previous battles had reopened, but he refused to withdraw and successfully bought time for his wounded comrades to reach friendly lines.

ON A BULLET- and explosion-riddled hill in Korea, Jack Weinstein volunteered to stay behind to cover the withdrawal of his platoon's wounded against a large force of counterattacking Chinese Communists. Born on December 6,

1928, in St. Francis, Kansas, Weinstein grew up in Oregon before returning to Kansas to live with his sister and her husband, Joyce and Floyd Carmichael, and to work on their farm. In 1948 he moved with his parents to Lamar, Missouri, where they were also engaged in farming. Drafted into the US Army in January 1950, Weinstein trained at Fort Leonard Wood, Missouri, before joining Company G, 2nd Battalion, 21st Infantry Regiment, 24th Infantry Division in Korea.

In the combat zone Weinstein rapidly rose in rank from private to sergeant. Early in his tour, shortly after his birthday in 1950, Weinstein wrote a letter home to his parents that was published in the local paper after he earn his first Purple Heart:

> Dear Mom and Dad, Received my birthday package today. The cake was swell, kinda flat when it got here, but still good. Think we are getting relieved today. Hope so any way. I went back to the line the other day, fell off a cliff and twisted my knee yesterday, so am back down again. I can't walk on it so there must be something wrong somewhere. If it isn't better in the morning I will turn into the medic. My arm is still a little stiff but I think it will be all right soon. Man, we got cut up this time, there are eight men left out of my platoon. Most of them just had small wounds but still they were hit and I had to watch them go off the hill. A lot of boys were crying, all broke up. If I had a brother, I know I wouldn't have been any closer to him than I was to my men. Don't know if I can stand this much longer myself. I know I am a grown boy but had to cry a little myself last night myself.

A year later, on October 19, 1951, Weinstein was a veteran infantryman participating with his company as a part of Operation Nomad near Kumsong. Their mission was to push the North Koreans and their Chinese Communist ally northward. An article in the January 1, 1952, edition of *Stars and Stripes* described the action:

> In the early stages of the offensive, Weinstein was a member of a leading platoon that had just secured an important hill after beating off the Reds in a brisk firefight. Many of the platoon had been hit and only a few soldiers were left to dig in and protect the hard won objective. Laboriously the soldiers gave aid to the wounded and also tried to set up a defense. Suddenly the men heard shouting defiant voices of the enemy in the valley below. A chorus of machineguns, small arms, and mortars filled the air. "Here they come," shouted the soldiers. The soldiers peered down at the

attacking enemy and answered the fire. Men stared down, hypnotized by the overwhelming number of enemy rushing over the hill. Then the order was given to withdraw. Weinstein volunteered to stay behind and cover the withdrawal of the rest of the platoon.

He fired continuously at the enemy forces, while the wounded were helped down the hill. Some turned to look at the lone figure for a moment and then move on. "I didn't think much of being alone up there," he said. "All I knew was that I must slow the Reds down."

Red after Red fell before the rapid fire from the lone defender. "Just when I started slowing them down I ran out of ammo," he said, "so I started using abandoned enemy grenades that littered the hill top."

Then an explosion deafened his ears and he felt a dull pain in his side; he'd been hit by a grenade fragment. His sight grew hazy and spots floated before his eyes. Moments passed before his sight returned and then he could see the wave of enemy soldiers surging towards him. He grasped several grenades and flung them down, tearing wide gaps in the howling wave. The game would soon be over, he thought, then someone began firing from the hilltop and more Reds fell. Glancing to the side he saw several soldiers firing at the enemy who turned tail and retreated. Relieving forces had arrived. He sank to the ground, his side was numb and he was tired, dog-tired. He had a smile on his face though; he knew he was going to make it.

For his actions on the hill, Weinstein received the Distinguished Service Cross and his second Purple Heart. He recovered from his wounds, was discharged, and returned to Lamar, where he married Nancy Nadine Rakestraw, whom he had met before the war. The Weinsteins returned to Jack's hometown of St. Francis, where he farmed and had a second job as a truck driver that included carrying dynamite. They had four sons and a daughter.

Weinstein died on April 20, 2006, after a lengthy illness. His services were held in the First Christian Church in St. Francis and he is buried in the nearby Cheyenne Valley Cemetery in Wheeler. His family and friends remember him for his happy nature, warm smile, and witty remarks.

The 2014 review of DSC recipients included Weinstein as one of twenty-four to have their award upgraded to the Medal of Honor. Nancy Weinstein accepted the medal from Pres. Barack Obama in a White House ceremony. She said that her husband did not talk much about the war and rarely showed his emotions but that he had no regrets and felt that it was his duty to serve.

Because of his name, many in the press and among the public believed Weinstein to be a Jew. Such is not the case. In an interview with the *Hays Daily News,* Nancy Weinstein said, "His family is German heritage, but they've never been any Jewish that I am aware of." Weinstein's Medal of Honor headstone contains the Latin cross.

On June 20, 2014, the town of St. Francis paid special tribute, "Honoring a Hero," to Weinstein in Sawhill Park. The town's mayor, Scott Schultz, presided.

SOURCES

The primary source for documents is the Congressional Medal of Honor (CMOH) Society and Museum, located on the USS *Yorktown* in Charleston Harbor at Mount Pleasant, South Carolina. The society's archives include all or part of individual enlistment records, birth and death certificates, obituaries, news articles, photographs, and other information. Its staff was most helpful in making these records available and in assisting in their review and reproduction.

It is worth noting that some of this information is not consistent in dates and locations and even, on occasion, in the basic facts themselves. This is all that much more true when one turns to the internet for search of Medal of Honor recipients. The first entry that usually comes up is on Wikipedia. Most of these citations are fairly accurate; however, there are mistakes and website after website merely repeats the facts and errors with no checking for accuracy.

What is contained in this book is information from the CHOH files and the sources cited in the following bibliography as well as personal interviews by telephone and email with surviving family members, local historians, and reference librarians in the recipients' hometowns. The author's experience from a twenty-year career as a US Army officer also greatly assisted in analyzing and interpreting the data.

Sadly, much information about Medal of Honor recipients of all races and religious preference has been lost to the passage of time and the fog of war—especially of their prewar experiences. It has only been in the past thirty years or so that concentrated efforts have been made to properly identify the graves of recipients and to gather information beyond their basic service records and

Medal of Honor citations. Further complicating research was the fire at the National Personal Records Center in St. Louis, Missouri, on July 12, 1973, that destroyed an estimated 16–18 million records of military veterans—including many of those of Medal of Honor recipients.

BOOKS

Adjutant General's Office, US War Department. *Chronological List of Actions, Etc., with Indians from January 15, 1837 to January 1891.* Fort Collins, CO: Old Army Press, 1979.

Anderson, John B. *The Fifty-Seventh Regiment of Massachusetts Volunteers in the War of the Rebellion, Army of the Potomac.* Boston: E. B. Shillings, 1896.

Ayling, Augustus D. *Revised Register of the Soldiers and Sailors of New Hampshire in the War of Rebellion, 1861–1866.* Concord, NH: Ira C. Evans, 1895.

Beyer, W. F., and O. F. Keydel, eds. *Deeds of Valor from the Records of the Archives of the United States Government: How American Heroes Won the Medal of Honor.* 2 vols. Detroit, MI: Perrien-Keydel, 1906.

Bielakowski, Alexander M. *Ethnic and Racial Minorities in the U.S. Military: An Encyclopedia.* 2 vols. Santa Barbara, CA: ABC-CLIO, 2013.

Blatner, David, and Ted Falcon. *Judaism for Dummies.* Hoboken, NJ: John Wiley & Sons, 2013.

Broadwater, Robert P. *Civil War Medal of Honor Recipients.* Jefferson, NC: McFarland, 2007.

Carroll, John. *The Medal of Honor: Its History and Recipients for the Indian Wars.* Bryan, TX: John Carroll, 1979.

Chester, Henry Whipple. *Recollections of the War of the Rebellion: A Story of the 2nd Ohio Volunteer Cavalry, 1861–1865.* Wheaton, IL: Wheaton History Center, 1996.

Cohen, Daniel M. *Single Handed: The Inspiring Story of Tibor "Teddy" Rubin—Holocaust Survivor, Korean War Hero, and Medal of Honor Recipient.* New York: Berkley Caliber, 2015.

Donovan, Frank R. *The Medal: The Story of the Medal of Honor.* New York: Dodd Meade, 1961.

Dyer, Frederick Henry. *A Compendium of the War of the Rebellion.* Des Moines, IA: Dyer Publishing, 1908.

Gause, Isaac. *Four Years with Five Armies: Army of the Frontier, Army of the Potomac, Army of the Missouri, Army of the Ohio, Army of the Shenandoah.* New York: Neale Publishing, 1908.

Gumpertz, Sydney G. *The Jewish Legion of Valor: The Story of Jewish Heroes in the Wars of the Republic.* New York: Sydney G. Gumpertz, 1934.

Hallas, James H. *Uncommon Valor on Iwo Jima: The Stories of the Medal of Honor Recipients in the Marine Corps' Bloodiest Battle of World War II.* Mechanicsburg, PA: Stackpole, 2016.

Hooper, James. *Medals of Honor.* New York: John Day, 1929.

Isaacs, Edouard Victor Michael. *Prisoner of the U-90.* New York: Houghton Mifflin, 1919.

Jackman, Lyman. *History of the Sixth New Hampshire Regiment in the War for the Union.* Concord, NH: Republican Press, 1891.

Jacobs, Bruce. *Heroes of the Army: The Medal of Honor and Its Winners.* New York: W. W. Norton, 1956.

Jacobs, Jack, and Douglas Century. *If Not Now, When? Duty and Sacrifice in America's Time of Need.* New York: Berkley Caliber, 2008.

Jacobs, Jack, and David Fisher. *Basic: Surviving Boot Camp and Basic Training.* New York: Thomas Dunne, 2012.

Jordan, Kenneth N. *Forgotten Heroes: 131 Men of the Korean War Awarded the Medal of Honor, 1950–1953.* Atglen, PA: Schiffer Publishing, 1995.

———. *Heroes of Our Time: 231 Men of the Vietnam War Awarded the Medal of Honor, 1964-1972.* Atglen, PA: Schiffer Publishing, 2004.

Kirk, Hyland Clare. *Heavy Guns and Light: A History of the 4th New York Heavy Artillery.* New York: C. T. Dillingham, 1890.

Korn, Bertran W. *American Jewry and the Civil War.* Philadelphia: Jewish Publication Society, 1951.

Lang, George, Raymond L. Collins, and Gerard F. White. *Medal of Honor Recipients, 1863–1994.* 2 vols. New York: Facts on File, 1995.

Laskin, David. *The Long Way Home: An American Journey from Ellis Island to the Great War.* New York: HarperCollins, 2010.

Love, Edmund G. *War Is a Private Affair.* New York: Harcourt Brace, 1959.

Mikaelian, Allen. *Medal of Honor: Profiles of America's Military Heroes from the Civil War to the Present.* New York: Hyperion, 2002.

Miles, L. Wardlaw. *History of the 308th Infantry, 1917–1919.* New York: Knickerbocker Press, 1927.

Mitchell, Joseph B. *The Badge of Gallantry: Recollections of Civil War Congressional Medal of Honor Winners.* New York: Macmillan, 1968.

Mulholland, St. Clair A. *Military Order Congress Medal of Honor Legion of the United States.* Philadelphia: Town Printing, 1905.

Murphy, Edward F. *Heroes of World War II.* Novato, CA: Presidio Press, 1990.

———. *Korean War Heroes.* Novato, CA: Presidio Press, 1992.

———. *Vietnam Medal of Honor Heroes.* Novato, CA: Presidio Press, 1997.

Nofi, Albert A. *Marine Corps Books of Lists: A Definitive Compendium of Marine Corps Feats, Facts, and Traditions.* Boston: DaCapo Press, 1999.

Noyes, Elmer Edward. *A History of the Grand Army of the Republic in Ohio from 1866 to 1900.* Columbus: Ohio State University Press, 1945.

Owens, Ronald J. *Medal of Honor: Historical Facts and Figures.* Paducah, KY: Turner Publishing, 2004.

Pinney, N. A. *History of the 104th Regiment Ohio Volunteer Infantry from 1862–1865.* Akron, OH: Werner & Lohmann, 1886.

Proft, Robert J. *United States of America's Congressional Medal of Honor Recipients: Their Official Citations.* Columbia Heights, MN: Highland House, 2007.

Reid, Whitelaw. *Ohio in the War: Her Statesmen, Her Generals, and Soldiers.* Cincinnati, OH: Moore, Wilstach & Baldwin, 1868.

Rigg, Bryan Mark. *Flamethrower: Iwo Jima Medal of Honor Recipient and U.S. Marine Woody Williams and His Controversial Award.* Addison, TX: Fidelis Historia, 2020.

Rosen, Robert N. *The Jewish Confederates.* Columbia: University of South Carolina Press, 2000.

Sarna, Jonathan D. and Adam Mendelsohn. *Jews and the Civil War.* New York: New York University Press, 2010.

Sawicki, James A. *Infantry Regiments of the U.S. Army.* Dumfries, VA: Wyvern Publications, 1981.

Schott, Joseph D. *Above and Beyond: The Story of the Congressional Medal of Honor.* New York: G. P. Putnam's Sons, 1963.

Schwartz, Laurens R. *Jews and the American Revolution: Haym Solomon and Others.* Jefferson, NC: McFarland, 1987.

Scott, Douglas. *Custer's Heroes: The Little Bighorn Medals of Honor.* Wake Forest, NC: AST Press, 2007.

Simonhoff, Harry. *Jewish Participants in the Civil War.* New York: ARCO, 1963.

Taggart, Donald G. *The History of the Third Infantry Division in World War II.* Washington, DC: Infantry Journal Press, 1947.

Tillman, Barrett. *Heroes: U.S. Army Medal of Honor Recipients.* New York: Berkley Group, 2006.

Wiernik, Peter. *History of the Jews in America.* New York: Jewish Press Publishing, 1912.

Wildolph, Charles. *I Fought with Custer: The Story of Sergeant Wildolph, Last Survivor of the Battle of the Little Big Horn.* Lincoln: University of Nebraska Press, 1987.

Wilkinson, Warren. *Mother, May You Never See the Sights I Have Seen: The Fifty-Seventh Massachusetts Veteran Volunteers in the Army of the Potomac, 1864–1865.* New York: Morrow, 1990.

Winegarten, Ruthe, and Cathy Schechter. *Deep in the Heart of Texas: The Lives and Legends of Texas Jews.* Austin, TX: Eakin Press, 1990.

Wolf, Simon. *The American Jew as Patriot, Soldier, and Citizen.* Philadelphia: Levytype, 1895.

Zickel, Lewis L. *The Jews of West Point*. Brooklyn, NY: KTAV Publishing House, 2009.

PERIODICALS

"A Salute to Heroes." *American Legion Magazine*. March 2013.

Applebaum, Emanuel. "Second Lieutenant Raymond Zussman—Congressional Medal of Honor." *Michigan Jewish History*. March 1961.

Bernatsky, Michelle, and Joan Alpert. "Anatomy of a Hero." *Jewish Veteran* 37, no 5 (July–August 1983): 8–9.

Blackman, Joyce. "A Civil War Hero and His Rhode Island Family Leopold Karpeles." *Rhode Island Jewish Historical Notes*. November 1995.

Correll, John T. "20 Seconds over Long Binh." *Air Force Magazine*. September 2010.

Diner, Hasia R. "Civil War in the United States." Jewish Women: A Comprehensive Historical Encyclopedia, February 27, 2009. Jewish Women's Archive. https://jwa.org/encyclopedia/article/civil-war-in-united-states.

Frisbee, John L. "The Saving of Spooky 71." *Air Force Magazine*. October 1984.

Knittel, Collette. "Dentist Hero Finally Awarded Congressional Medal of Honor." *Journal of the California Dental Association*. September 2002.

Laskin, David. "William Shemin Gets His Medal of Honor—a Century Later." *Forward*. June 21, 2015.

"MOH Recipient Dedicates AC-47." *VAnguard*. May 1984.

Murphy, Edward R. "Corporal Samuel Gross: Congressional Medal of Honor, Awarded September 17, 1917." *Jewish Veteran*. April–June 1982.

"New Veterans Health Center Named for Medal of Honor Recipient SGT John Lee Levitow." *Jewish Veteran*. June 2008.

Pizer, Vernon. "Medal of Honor: Vignettes of Courage." *American Legion Magazine*. November 1987.

Plante, Trevor K. "U.S. Marines in the Boxer Rebellion." *Prologue*. Winter 1999.

"Posthumous Medal of Honor for WW I 4ID Veteran." *Ivy Leaves*. Fall 2015.

Shosteck, Robert. "Jewish Heroes in Blue and Gray." *Jewish Criterion*. September 22, 1959.

Tiron, Roxana. "Army Training Site Brings to Life the Horrors of War." *National Defense*. July 2001.

Twain, Mark. "Concerning the Jews." *Harper's Magazine* 99, no. 592 (September 1899): 527 535.

INDEX

ABOUT THE AUTHOR

MICHAEL LEE LANNING is the author of more than two dozen nonfiction books on military history, sports, and health. More than 1.1 million copies of his books are in print in fifteen countries, and editions have been translated into twelve languages. He has appeared on major television networks and the History Channel as an expert on the individual soldier on both sides of the Vietnam War.

The New York Times Book Review declared Lanning's *Vietnam 1969–1970: A Company Commander's Journal* to be "one of the most honest and horrifying accounts of a combat soldier's life to come out of the Vietnam War." The *London Sunday Times* devoted an entire page to review his *The Military 100: A Ranking of the Most Influential Military Leaders of All Time.* According to the *San Francisco Journal*, Lanning's *Inside the VC and NVA* is "a well-researched, groundbreaking work that fills a huge gap in the historiography of the Vietnam War."

A veteran of more than twenty years in the US Army, Lanning is a retired lieutenant colonel. During the Vietnam War he served as an infantry platoon leader, reconnaissance platoon leader, and an infantry company commander. In addition to having earned the Combat Infantryman's Badge and the Bronze Star with "V" device with two oak leaf clusters, Lanning is Ranger-qualified and a senior parachutist.

Lanning was born in Sweetwater, Texas, and is a 1964 graduate of Trent High School. He has a BS from Texas A&M University and an MS from East Texas State University. He currently resides in Lampasas, Texas.

BOOKS BY MICHAEL LEE LANNING

The Only War We Had: A Platoon Leader's Journal of Vietnam
Vietnam 1969-1970: A Company Commander's Journal
Inside the LRRPs: Rangers in Vietnam
Inside Force Recon: Recon Marines in Vietnam (with Ray W. Stubbe)
The Battles of Peace
Inside the VC and NVA: The Real Story of North Vietnam's Armed Forces
    (with Dan Cragg)
Vietnam at the Movies
Senseless Secrets: The Failures of US Military Intelligence, from
    George Washington to the Present
The Military 100: A Ranking of the Most Influential Military Leaders of All Time
The African American Soldier: From Crispus Attucks to Colin Powell
Inside the Crosshairs: Snipers in Vietnam
Defenders of Liberty: African Americans in the Revolutionary War
Blood Warriors: American Military Elites
The Battle 100: The Stories behind History's Most Influential Battles
Mercenaries: Soldiers of Fortune, from Ancient Greece to Today's Private
    Military Companies
The Civil War 100: The Stories behind the Most Influential Battles, People, and
    Events in the War Between the States
The Revolutionary War 100: The Stories behind the Most Influential Battles,
    People, and Events of the American Revolution
Double T Double Cross: The Firing of Coach Mike Leach
At War with Cancer (with Linda Moore-Lanning)
Tours of Duty: Vietnam War Stories
Tony Buzbee: Defining Moments
Texas Aggies in Vietnam: War Stories
The Veterans Cemeteries of Texas
Dear Allyanna: An Old Soldier's Last Letter to His Granddaughter
The Court Martial of Jackie Robinson
The Blister Club: The Extraordinary Story of the Downed American Airmen
    Who Escaped to Safety in World War II

CPSIA information can be obtained
at www.ICGtesting.com
Printed in the USA
LVHW081356150422
716126LV00002B/2